FROM THE LION'S MOUTH

FROM THE LION'S MOUTH

Healing from
Trauma, Electroshock, Scapegoating, and Grief
in a Dysfunctional Family and Psychiatric System

JULIA HOEFFLER WELTON

ISBN-13: 978-1502521149
ISBN-10: 1502521148

Library of Congress Control Number: 2014917376

CreateSpace Independent Publishing Platform, North Charleston, SC

Book and cover design by Karl Gerlach, http://translationstudio.de.
Original cover photograph by Flickr user "coloredby," altered from
https://www.flickr.com/photos/74881150@N00/5649525348,
licensed through Creative Commons Attribution 2.0.

Printed in the United States of America.

To my husband, Tom,
who rescued me from the lion's mouth and
to all who by helping and healing others contribute
to the redemption of the world.

The Last Word

Creep into thy narrow bed,
Creep, and let no more be said!
Vain thy onset! all stands fast.
Thou thyself must break at last.

Let the long contention cease!
Geese are swans, and swans are geese.
Let them have it how they will!
Thou art tired: best be still.

They out-talked thee, hissed thee, tore thee?
Better men fared thus before thee;
Fired their ringing shot and passed,
Hotly charged – and sank at last.

Charge once more, then, and be dumb!
Let the victors, when they come,
When the forts of folly fall,
Find thy body by the wall!

– Matthew Arnold

TABLE OF CONTENTS

Acknowledgements

This book would never have been written without the encouragement of Irini and her sister Despina, who for more than forty years urged me to write my story. Another *sine qua non* is Tom, my cherished husband, who deserves many thanks for his unfailing support of the project. I also wish to thank my dear friends who read the manuscript and offered helpful and perceptive comments: Judith, Beverly, Cathie, Jane, Jocelynn, Peggy, Despina, Irini, and M.A. and her husband Jim. And to Karl, boundless gratitude for his patient editing and formatting work and for designing the cover.

Author's Note

There are no fictitious persons or events in this book. In some instances I have changed names in order to respect the privacy of persons still living.

For reasons that will become obvious to the reader, I consistently use the abbreviation EST and the term electroshock rather than the medical establishment's euphemism, electroconvulsive therapy (ECT).

PREFACE

Every day I walked to class as a graduate student at the University of Texas at Austin, I would pass the Main Building with its landmark tower. Chiseled in two-foot letters into its limestone façade are words from the Gospel of John: *Ye shall know the truth and the truth shall make you free.* These words became a reminder of my quest: to discover the truth about what happened to me many years earlier and to be free of the ongoing pain it caused.

Every person has a life story worth telling and writing; not everyone has the means or opportunity to do so. I am grateful I can set out in these pages the history of my strange yet ordinary and unremarkable life. Many people have had more difficult and painful lives, yet mine was the life I lived, and I feel it is important to acknowledge publicly what happened to me. I am grateful to see my memoir published, and thus not remain in a category of victims Azar Nafisi defines as those "who have no defense and are never given a chance to articulate their own story." A victim of this kind, notes Nafisi, "becomes a double victim: not only her life but also her life story is taken from her."[1]

At age sixty-seven, shame and fear no longer dominate my life. The people who hurt me are all dead, and I continue to be healed from the traumas I endured more than forty years ago. My life is a triple miracle: 1) it is a miracle that I am alive; 2) it is a double miracle that I am not locked away somewhere, my mind destroyed; 3) it is a triple miracle that I have had something of a career and have been a partner in a stable, loving marriage of thirty-eight years.

I am writing in some haste, after a diagnosis of cancer in May 2013, followed by eight months of rigorous, and so far successful, treatment. This brush with mortality makes chronicling these events all the more urgent.

For more than forty years, friends have encouraged me to write my story, but until now I've always felt too afraid of being stigmatized to reveal the truth. After a relatively happy childhood, I found myself in a family that became increasingly dysfunctional as my parents' drinking developed into alcoholism. My mother, misinterpreting normal teenage development and symptoms of mononucleosis, took me to a psychiatrist who victimized me with electroshock treatments for almost four years. Rescued through a stroke of fate I still don't comprehend, I managed to complete my education and carve out a career as I sought and found healing from many different sources.

In essence, my quest for healing and understanding has been a religious one. Beginning with writings in psychology, psychiatry and philosophy, I found concepts that could name certain experiences as objective facts, but not the underlying truth I was seeking. I ultimately found the means to understand my experience of victimization when I began exploring the question of forgiveness within the paradigm – and community – of the Christian faith.

Verifying the truth of remembered events and their sequence – what actually happened and when – was a different challenge. Conversations with friends and family members who had known me since I was a child confirmed that my memories were indeed true. My personal medical records and correspondence, excerpts of which I cite in this memoir, supplied another source. I was then slowly able to piece together a coherent narrative of what had happened to me. This book is both record and result of that process.

My hope is that this book may in some way help those who have survived similar experiences. It is also my hope that publishing this book will be an act of justice and will help me find closure and peace from the continuing pain of what happened more than forty years ago.

PROLOGUE: FAMILIES

Happy families are all alike; every unhappy family
is unhappy in its own way.

–Leo Tolstoy, *Anna Karenina*

A snapshot taken in 1947 shows my mother sitting outdoors on a straight-backed chair, gingerly holding her infant daughter on her lap. She's wearing a flowered print dress, her brown hair braided tightly about her head. Mother's posture is rigid, as if the picture taking were an intrusion. In a white smock, I lie on my back, crying, looking up at my mother's face. She sits sideways to the camera, unsmiling, her arms tense as she leans awkwardly toward her child.

"The diaphragm didn't work," my mother explained when I was in my teens. "We wanted another child," she said, "but not just then." I wasn't my parents' first child. My father finished a PhD in biochemistry in 1946 at the University of Michigan in Ann Arbor, where my brother was born. With their infant son they returned to Texas, to Galveston, where Dad joined the faculty of the medical school and Mother taught in the public schools. One year later I was born.

In their student days my parents, Bill and Laura, had hoped for a great future. Dad dreamed of a Nobel Prize for discovering a cure for cancer, but his career stalled as research came no closer to an answer and funding was scarce. Mother, who had envisioned herself a keen investigative reporter traveling across Europe with her typewriter case, was anchored to the American South, a careworn housewife with a new baby and a toddler barely out of diapers.

As youthful dreams faded, their drinking became habitual. By the time they moved to Houston in 1948 for my father to take a research position as a biochemist at MD Anderson, several beers a night and the occasional cocktail flowed into a normal pattern. Most often submerged under routines of work and childcare, fault lines were beginning to show in their marriage, and alcohol helped keep them hidden.

At four years old, I had learned by heart several of the bedtime books Mother read to me. Once during their evening drinks, I proudly brought in one of my favorites and began to "read" it aloud. Now on his second beer of the evening, my father handed me an unfamiliar book. "Can you read this?" he asked.

Another evening I wanted to show I had learned to write. Bringing in a piece of paper and a crayon, I spelled out the one word "HOP" I had somehow learned to print. My dad gave me a fresh piece of paper. "Can you spell *elephant*?" he teased.

The next day I took my crayons and wrote H-O-P in large letters all over the dining room walls. When Mother discovered my handiwork, she gave me a hard spanking, dragging me into the dining room and scolding me for what I had done.

One night after everyone was asleep, my mother and father were awakened by screams from my bedroom. Following one school of expert advice, my parents believed in letting a child cry itself out and learn to comfort itself. But this time the crying was so loud and lasted so long that they both came to check on me, reassuring me and getting me settled back into bed.

The next morning was a Saturday, and my father, working in the yard, found my bedroom window screens lying against the wall. The neighbors told him that there had been several burglaries that night. He called the police, who came to the house and dusted for fingerprints on my windowsill. Afraid the police were after me, I hid behind my mother as she answered their questions.

"You'd make a good watchdog," my father said later. "You scared the burglar away!" I could hear the love in his voice.

My parents didn't usually have much love in their voices, especially after they had consumed the first one or two drinks of the evening. At the dinner table my father would complain about his job at the research center and then start in on my brother and me. Tired, frustrated, or depressed, Mother usually had neither time nor patience for me. "I don't want to fool with you!" was a frequent response to my requests for attention.

❖

Grandpa Miller, my mother's father, seemed the only adult who was ever glad to see me. Two or three times a year my mother would take the Santa Fe night train to Ballinger, with my brother and me in tow. I still remember the gentle sounds and sway of the train and the large snaps on the velvet curtains of the sleeper bunks.

The best part of the visits was Grandpa. When we got off the train, Grandpa and Grandma would be waiting on the platform. Grandpa would reach down, pick me up and kiss me – his face radiant at seeing his granddaughter.

With me next to him on the front seat, Grandpa would drive us home. One of the largest in town, their two-story house had majestic white columns, its substantial veranda complete with a swing and wooden rocking chairs, painted white. Grandma would have sandwiches and fresh lemonade ready for us, and we would waste no time unpacking and making ourselves at home.

I loved Grandpa and all but worshipped him. Victor Miller was tall and strong, a rip-roarin' Texan type, full of energy and good humor, loud and full of life. A lawyer and a rancher, he had often handled cases during the Depression for no fee or in exchange for a day's work in the yard or on the ranch.

In 1904 when he was a boy of fourteen, his left leg was badly crushed in a buggy accident. He would have died, but the need for tetanus serum was telegraphed to Austin on a new line just put through. The serum was hurried onto a train in a bucket of ice and sent to Ballinger. He did not die, but his leg couldn't be saved. Neither the missing leg nor the pain he still experienced slowed him down. He fished, swam, danced, roller-skated, and even went to Korea as a civilian volunteer to help after the war.

One of my mother's brothers wrote a poem about him after he died:

On a leg that was good
And one made of wood
Like a giant he stood.
Equaled by few
None greater I knew
On legs that were true.

Riding in the pickup on the ranch under the West Texas sky, I was full of joy just to be with him. I was his favorite – he always picked me up and hugged and kissed me before he greeted the grownups. I loved it when he swooped me up in his strong arms and I felt his stubbly cheek against my own.

In the summer of 1954 I had just turned seven years old. My father, dissatisfied with his work at the research center, was looking for a new job, and Mother and Dad had also planned an August vacation at a fishing camp on the Llano River. News came before we left Houston that Grandpa had been injured in a car accident in Austin.

Bypassing the fishing camp, we drove straight to Ballinger. We trooped up the steps and lined up in the living room – Mother, Dad, my brother, and I. Grandma came in from the back hall, her face looking drawn and tired, and said a few quiet words to my mother and dad. I stood still, not listening, waiting for Grandpa. As he shuffled slowly into the room, Mother gripped my shoulder so tightly it hurt, stopping me from questioning, from running to him. Grandpa's eyes looked vacant. He did not recognize me.

For the two days the family stayed in Ballinger, I was afraid to approach Grandpa. As I was playing in the sandpile in the back yard, he came out on the porch and sat down in the swing at the side of the house. I remember holding my breath and sitting very still, watching him as he sat for a few minutes and then went back indoors as if he hadn't seen me.

During our week on the river, we fished for perch and bass. As we waited for the fish to bite, the sound of the water lapping against the boat was soothing under the hot sun. Late one night I woke up twice to the telephone ringing, though I stayed very still. I couldn't hear all the words, only muffled voices that meant the calls were serious. The next morning our parents told us both calls had been from Ballinger. The first had brought the news that my dad had been offered a new job in Birmingham, Alabama, as a professor of biochemistry at the university medical school. The second call told them Grandpa was dead.

We drove back to Ballinger so our parents could help Grandma make preparations for the funeral. Two of Mother's brothers came home with their families; her youngest brother was home from college on summer vacation. Mother had packed a suit for Dad and church clothes for her and the children – just in case.

At the funeral home, all I could do was hold my mother's hand. I kept my head down and couldn't look directly at Grandpa's body in the coffin. Later, at the funeral in the church, I stood up and sat down mechanically when my parents did, unable to sing the hymns or pay attention to the service.

I still remember the sound of the dry August grass underfoot as we made our way to the cars for the drive to the cemetery. People along the road stood still for the funeral procession driving by and the men along the way, especially on the streets in town, removed their hats as we passed.

The next day we drove north to Lockney, to the farm of my other grandparents. On the long drive through the flat, empty landscape I still felt numb. My other grandparents, however, had news of their own. They were retiring, selling the farm, and moving to Tulia, a small railroad and market town in the Texas Panhandle. Amid all the excitement about the move, the only person who noticed me was Grandmother Hoeffler, who said in her sweet voice, "You can remember Tulia, it rhymes with Julia."

Soon after returning to Houston, we moved to Birmingham and stayed for a couple of weeks in a small hotel. My brother and I played in the pool and enjoyed sliding down the small hill behind the hotel, but everything we did seemed to take place in a different world. I had lost Grandpa, the one person on earth who seemed to love and value me without disguised resentment.

After a few weeks at the hotel, the four of us moved into an apartment south of Birmingham and soon settled into a weekly routine. Our father took us to the public library once a week, and once assured we both loved to read, bought a small black and white television.

On Saturdays, my brother, who had to sleep on a sofabed in the living room, woke up early and turned on the TV. I woke up soon after and both of us got our own bowls of cereal and watch-ed the test pattern until the cartoons came on.

My parents joined a Presbyterian church we attended most every Sunday. During the week, my brother and I went to Shades Cahaba Elementary, while Dad carpooled on alternate days with colleagues.

Mother kept house, and on the days she had the car, attended church circle meetings or played bridge at friends' homes or the newly opened bridge club. She never told me why she had such a passion for the game, but it wasn't for the coffee, bridge prizes, and gossip. She became a keenly competitive player, earning points toward a Life Master in the American Contract Bridge League.

The next year my parents bought a steep hillside lot from a homebuilder who offered a choice of floor plans and décor. One Saturday Dad drove us to the building site and my brother and I had fun exploring the bare floor and frame that would become our new home. My brother would now have his own room and our parents' bedroom would have its own bathroom: a luxury after the cramped apartment.

Some of my fondest childhood memories come from the six years we lived in that house. Dad planted herbs where a terrace retaining wall made a waist-high garden, and I planted a small vegetable garden outside my bedroom window. Dad was puzzled that my carrots weren't thriving until he discovered I was pulling them up periodically to check their progress.

My room had a double bed with a bookcase headboard I filled with books. I arranged my stuffed animals on the bed. Along one wall was the dollhouse Grandpa had built for me, where my col-lection of nested wooden dolls lived. Sleepyville, the name I gave this community of toys, included Chinatown, where my glazed pottery animals sat on their own shelf. I played with them for hours, even having them hold an election, with little squares of paper on which every single one voted. Bear Snizzups, one of the Chinatown figures, won the election and became Mayor of Sleepyville.

The front door opened onto a small porch, high above the yard, at the top of a long set of brick steps running across the front of the house. My friend Beverly and I invented a game of tying ropes under the arms of our teddy bears and pitching them towards the grass below. We would reel them back in and let them fly as often as they wanted, talking for them in our bear voices about how they enjoyed each flight.

With a higher income and the new house constructed, my parents could now afford vodka and vermouth. They drank martinis like Nick and Nora in the 1930s Thin Man movies I saw on TV, and one or two drinks a night turned into three. Ever the chemist, Dad didn't use a pitcher, but mixed the martinis in a tall thermos, twisting the handle of a long spoon through a strainer.

After two or three drinks, sometimes four, my parents became more distant, less themselves. Dad's teasing would begin, and criticism of work, each other, or the children would fill most of the evening. My mother would sit quietly, judging the conversation as she might evaluate a hand of bridge, then interject a few critical remarks of her own. I only realized later why I would stiffen whenever I heard the sound of the swirling ice clinking against the spoon.

When I was ten, my mother had a "nervous breakdown," as my aunt described it many years later. My mother wanted to divorce my dad, my aunt said, because she "couldn't stand it anymore." But Mother didn't file for divorce; instead, she called Grandma Miller to come out from Texas and take care of my brother and me while she played bridge away from home.

When I learned Grandma was coming and would share my room for a six-week visit, I was so excited that I couldn't stop talking about it, and after she finally arrived I barely noticed the change in the family dynamic. Dad and Mother had fewer drinks and spoke more reasonably to each other, and Mother seemed more relaxed.

Grandma and I would read the Bible together before going to bed, and she would tell me stories about her childhood in La Grange, Texas. She was born in 1896 and had three sisters. Laura, the sister for whom my mother was named, had died at age nineteen after a birthday party, as the story goes, from swallowing a pin in the decorations.

She also reminisced about how Grandpa had asked her to marry him the first night they met, at a dance in Bellville. Sitting on the porch swing, Grandpa was surprised when it started shaking after he proposed. He thought Grandma was crying with emotion, while actually she was laughing, since they had only just met and others had told her that Victor might ask her to marry him that first night. She refused him that evening, but she was taken with the forthright young man and their courtship continued to marriage in 1916.

I always missed Grandpa. Every night I prayed "Now I lay me down to sleep" and added many petitions, thanking God for each family member by name – all the aunts, uncles, and cousins – and asking God to bless each one, again by name. The bedtime prayer finished with: "Please don't let the Russians come over, and please don't let any bombs be dropped anywhere," and the most important prayer of all, "And please let me get to kiss and hug Grandpa Miller one more time."

Mother "battled the budget," as she said, with ferocious control and every summer managed to send my brother and me away to camp and for visits to Grandma in Texas. My brother and I didn't always get along well and Mother felt it wise to keep us separated as much as possible during the long summer months. I would be sent to camp while my brother visited Grandma in Ballinger, and my brother went to camp while I visited Grandma.

On my first visit, Mother and Dad drove me to the Birmingham airport and handed me over to the stewardess at the gate. In case I missed the flight change in Houston, Mother had pinned my spending money and a note with names and phone numbers on my dress so someone could get me safely to Ballinger. My aunt and uncle picked me up at the San Angelo airport. Years later, my aunt remembered how cute I looked dressed up in traveling clothes with my long braids.

This was the year after Grandpa died. One afternoon, Grandma and I went to the cemetery to water the grass and put fresh flowers on Grandpa's grave. I knew he was lying under the earth beneath the grey granite stone, but I listened instead to the sound of the wind in the juniper trees nearby.

I filled the long summer days at Grandma's playing with my uncle's dogs, roller skating on the front sidewalk, or when it was too hot to do anything else, sitting in one of the rocking chairs, listening to Grandma talk about family history as she fanned herself with a cardboard fan. The porch ceiling was painted light blue. This was to keep wasps from building nests, Grandma said, since they would be fooled into thinking it was the sky.

Sometimes my uncle, a veterinarian, took me along to the ranch in the pickup. He once showed me how to milk the cow Grandma still kept. I was trying to be gentle, but all of a sudden she swished her tail right in my face. "She's just nervous being milked by someone new," my uncle reassured me.

These idyllic visits to Ballinger were something I looked forward to every year. Grandma always let me eat my favorite foods. When she made her famous lemon ice cream, my favorite, I would turn the crank of the ice cream freezer on the back steps. This was not lemon custard, she insisted, but lemon *ice cream,* demanding special handling to keep it from curdling on the stove.

When it was my turn to go to camp, I went to Camp Coleman, a Girl Scout camp near Birmingham. Unlike home, it was a place where things happened at predictable times and in predictable ways. We'd march down the dirt road under the trees to the meal hall, singing funny camp songs. Standing behind our chairs at the family style tables, we sang grace before sitting down for the meal, where we joked, laughed and enjoyed the food. We even liked cleaning up afterward, washing dishes in big tubs rolled out on carts by the kitchen staff.

Toward the end of an evening around the campfire, we sang more serious songs: *Kum ba yah* – in those days still a camp song, not a cliché – or the round *Whene're you make a promise.* One song I particularly loved was also a round: "All things shall perish from under the sky. Music alone shall live, music alone shall live, music alone shall live, never to die."

On the last night we set little boats made of pine bark afloat in the river that ran through the camp. We made the little boats the day before, carving out a small hole for a candle. Groups of girls would walk onto the bridge after they had each placed their boats in the river. As we sang a song on the bridge, we watched our twinkling boats drift away. I was one of the girls who cried during this ritual of farewell, because I did not want to go home.

In music class at elementary school, our teacher, the concertmaster of the Birmingham Symphony, played LP recordings of orchestral music. Beethoven's "Emperor" piano concerto and his "Pastoral" and "Choral" symphonies were my favorites. Mr. Levinison made up words for us to sing to the melodies, and the class played the *Ode to Joy* on small plastic recorders. I was attracted to the oboe singing in the birdcalls of the "Pastoral," but even more to the piano's majestic role in the Emperor concerto. I began to beg my parents for a piano so I could play at home.

Mother rented a small upright piano from the E. E. Forbes Music Store and taught me the rudiments of music. By the middle of my third grade year, she realized I was serious about wanting to study music and arranged for me to have lessons with Mrs. Murray, our church organist. I looked forward to lessons and enjoyed practicing, especially the short Haydn and Beethoven pieces she gave me to learn. I even set my alarm clock early so I could practice half an hour before the school bus came.

The following years went by quickly, filled with experiences, funny and serious, sad and happy, challenging and exciting: trying to make butter with my brother by using the electric mixer on a bowl of buttermilk when I was nine, reciting from memory the list of sixty-one prepositions we had to learn for sixth grade, trying out my first high heels before my first dance wearing the beautiful green velvet dress Mother had sewn for me.

In 1961 our family moved up the same road to a larger house. As I turned to other interests, my dollhouse, with the characters of Sleepyville carefully packed away, moved to the attic. My parents had long since bought the upright piano they had rented for me. It stood along one living room wall until I turned sixteen, when it was traded in for a small grand piano, a much more responsive instrument to play the longer, more difficult pieces I had mastered.

The most important feature of the house for my father, however, was the hill on which it was built: a bomb shelter could be constructed below ground and out of sight from the road. Worried about the escalating threat of nuclear war with the Soviet Union, he consulted our minister about what to do if neighbors tried to force their way into the shelter. Should he shoot them if they did? The shelter only had enough food and water for the four weeks the government recommended, and the taking of human life, even in such dire circumstances, was not something he could contemplate alone.

When my mother told me about it later, her voice was laden with contempt for his seeking advice from the minister, even more for believing that Birmingham was in any real danger from Russian bombs or missiles. The whole idea was absurd, and she suspected this fraught concern, though encouraged by President Kennedy that very year,[2] signaled an underlying mental illness.

It fell to Mother, however, to keep the shelter stocked and rotate the foodstuffs every four weeks. My brother and I explored the shelter once, but it was cramped and uncomfortable. We couldn't imagine living cooped up with our parents for a month in such a dark, creepy place.

As the Cuban missile crisis faded from the news, no one mentioned the shelter much. Its exhaust pipe and ladder access in the back yard remained a silent reminder of the Cold War, but my dad no longer insisted on keeping it stocked. The people who later bought the house had it dug out and sold for scrap.

As my brother and I became teenagers, family conversations around the dinner table took a new turn: we became more willing to speak up and argue with our parents. With the first drinks of the evening, Mother and Dad could dull some of their mutual defensiveness, but drinks three and four – and now, sometimes five – only increased their unspoken rancor and bitterness. One evening in the car, Mother told me that when I was a baby and my brother only two, she had wanted to divorce Dad. "I could have made it on my own with one child," she said, "but I knew I could not have made it with two, and so I said to myself, God damn it, he begat these children, he is going to support them."

Mother's decision to stay with Dad was never final. Although she smoothed over her discontent in front of others, her wish to leave my father was a dark undertow in almost every interaction at home. As I grew older, more and more of her frustration with Dad rose to the surface, and I became at times her unwilling confidante.

Dad's frustration with work had grown more acute, and he had broken down when Mother had to have a biopsy for a lump she discovered in her left breast. It turned out to be benign, but Mother was convinced that Dad's intense fear that she might die was another sign of mental illness.

Mother's internist referred her to a psychiatrist, and Dad began to see Harold P. Larkin, a psychiatrist at a private mental hospital and a member of the clinical faculty at the University. Larkin diagnosed him as manic-depressive – an older term for what is now known as bi-polar disorder – and prescribed an early anti-depressant.[3] Dad accepted the diagnosis and took the drugs, but his drinking and two pack a day cigarette habit continued.

It later occurred to me that this diagnostic label freed him from any real responsibility for his behavior, both in his and Mother's eyes. My parents would never have considered counseling – it was, after all, only the early 1960s – and they did not realize, or could not admit to themselves, how much alcohol was poisoning their marriage.[4] The atmosphere in the Hoeffler house, as my friend Beverly remembered it much later, was "dark and dysfunctional."

1. Adolescence

There's only one thing harder than living in a home with an adolescent – and that's being an adolescent. The moodiness, the volatility, the wholesale lack of impulse control, all would be close to clinical conditions if they occurred at another point in life. In adolescence, they're just part of the behavioral portfolio.[5]

– Jeffery Kluger

The atmosphere at home was indeed dark and dysfunctional, even more so after the move to the house with the fallout shelter, and later, when my brother left for college.

My father sometimes defended himself against Mother's disdain by making outrageous puns, hoping to elicit a wry groan of acknowledgement from his wife. Other times he got angry without warning, cursing "God damn it to hell!" and smashing his fists on the table, car dashboard, or whatever flat surface was available.

The anti-depressants Larkin prescribed did not improve his moods. The dinner table remained conflicted and tense, and we ate late in the evening, about 9:00 or even later, because when Dad got home from work around 7:00, my mother and he sat and drank their martinis.

Dad was the cook in our house, and he took his time – drinking his martinis, reading the paper, and talking with Mother for a good two hours each night while preparing dinner. Mother complained about how many pots and pans he used, and the dishes were usually left to soak overnight until she washed them the next day. By the time I was a teenager, sometimes I would pour unfinished martinis down the sink when my parents had gone into the living room after dinner.

As I grew during the teenage years, an uncanny physical resemblance to my mother became apparent. Family friends who had known my mother as a girl would often tell me how much I looked like her, but even casual observers would comment on the strong resemblance. I tried to concentrate on the differences. Standing in my bedroom in front of the mirror, I mentally checked off the physical differences between us. I still remember the list: She had brown eyes, while my eyes were green. She was 5 foot 7 inches tall and I only 5 foot 4. She wore glasses, I did not… I did not want to be like her in any way.[6]

I continued piano with Mrs. Murray, squeezing in practice time when I could, while still trying to keep high grades in school. As my technique and musicianship improved, I played in annual recitals. Eventually I was chosen twice as a winner of the annual piano concerto competitions at the Alabama Music Teachers Association. With Mrs. Murray accompanying on a second piano, as a sophomore I played the Haydn D major concerto, and as a junior in high school I played Mendelssohn's Concerto in G minor.

As I listened to more orchestral music on the radio my yearning to play the oboe grew stronger. I was disappointed when I joined the junior high band and was told I first had to learn the clarinet for marching season. But I wanted to play the oboe so badly that learning enough of the clarinet to march didn't seem like an insurmountable obstacle. During the eighth grade, I took oboe lessons from Pasquale Bria at E. E. Forbes downtown, where I would climb three flights of dusty stairs to a small music room Mr. Bria rented. When my brother got his driver's license, he was drafted to take me to Saturday lessons with the oboe teacher at The University of Alabama in Tuscaloosa, sixty miles away.

After my brother left for college, Mother arranged for me to study oboe with Mr. Ronchetti, the oboist with the Birmingham Symphony, and I drove myself to lessons in Trussville, where he taught music in the high school. I felt drawn to Mr. and Mrs. Ronchetti – she played second oboe and English horn in the symphony – and their warm home, where Mr. Ronchetti gave me lessons in the kitchen, usually filled with the aroma of oregano and garlic.

Two musical instruments, honors English, Latin, French, and advanced math were a lot to manage at fifteen, and I fell ill with recurring sore throats, other respiratory symptoms, and stopped up ears. Some of this was probably related to my oboe playing, but the family doctor was unsure of a diagnosis, especially when he saw something suspicious in the blood sample.

Dad drove me to the University medical school lab for a thorough workup. In the car, he became very serious when I asked, "What do they think I have?" His hands tightened on the steering wheel and he spoke evenly, saying that there was something unusual about my white blood cell count the local doctor could not interpret.

"Do they think I have leukemia?" I asked.

"Yes," he answered.

It turned out to be two simultaneous diseases: mononucleosis and pneumonia. To cure the pneumonia, the doctor prescribed antibiotics; time and rest were the only treatment for mononucleosis.

In the fall of 1963, my brother enrolled in a college out of state, leaving me alone to absorb the teasing and goading my father dished out every night at the dinner table. I still had not learned to keep silent or ignore his taunts, but always tried to defend myself. Mother, feeling her martinis, sat at the table, barely speaking, observing us with cold irritation.

I began having trouble getting to sleep on weeknights. Dinner was so late and I couldn't get to my homework until my parents had turned in for the night; I often studied long past midnight, and then felt wide awake and unable to sleep. The next morning I could hardly lift my head from the pillow. This annoyed my mother, who had her own sleep problems and occasionally took prescription barbiturates.[7]

When my brother left for college, Mother went back to teaching school. Child of the Great Depression that she was, Mother knew the family needed more money to send two children to college at the same time. She was suffering from back pains and a difficult menopause, but she completed the night school classes required for Alabama certification, reviewed her German, and found a job teaching at a local high school.

In the spring of 1964 my mother was delighted to receive a fellowship from the Goethe Institute in Germany to study the language for six weeks that summer. I was accepted as an oboist to attend the prestigious Sewanee Summer Music Center in Tennessee. My father and brother, home from college, spent the summer together, camping and hunting.

At music camp, I fell in love for the first time – with a young cello student, Neal. I was shy with boys, but Neal, handsome with his blond hair and blue eyes, was intelligent and considerate. Waiting to audition for orchestra seats on the first day, we started a casual conversation and established an immediate rapport. We could talk easily about music, books, and impressions of the camp. But we also could talk about deeper things – plans for our future lives and our beliefs about God.

Neal gave me a birthday card and a small stuffed animal with soft white fur. The two of us were considered something of an item by the teachers and other students, who may have thought, incorrectly, that we were intimately involved. This was not the case because of my shyness, but Neal and I spent enough time alone together that they could have assumed more fiction than fact.

Shortly before camp was over, Neal and I discussed the future. Although we both lived in Birmingham, Neal went to a private school far from the high school I attended and we reconciled ourselves to being just friends, who would see each other once a month at youth orchestra rehearsals.

The school year began with a surprise. I had heard about the formidable senior honors English teacher, Miss Mackey. I had taken honors English as a junior, and knew the reading list would be even longer for a senior class. So I took a significant step towards independence: I lightened my schedule, signing up for less demanding courses to have time to practice the Beethoven G major, the concerto I had chosen as a competition piece.

On the first day of classes, I was one of a small group of seniors called to the principal's office. We were told that our scores on the National Merit Scholarship test had been outstanding and our schedules had been changed to include a course new to the school, advanced placement English – to be taught by Miss Mackey. This was the first year the school had offered advanced placement courses, and we weren't told we could refuse this honor.

Beethoven's G major concerto is a demanding work, both technically and musically. Mrs. Murray tried to dissuade me from attempting it, but I was determined. One reason was a private one. The second movement is a much discussed dialogue between the solo piano's soft pleading and the stern replies of the unison strings, often compared to Orpheus pleading with Pluto, the ruler of Hades, for the return of his beloved Eurydice.[8] Gradually the strings become softer and the piano plays more extended melodies. The strings' responses become shorter and softer as Pluto is won over to let Eurydice return. When Orpheus looks back to see if she is following, all hope is lost, and the movement concludes poignantly as she sinks back into the underworld realm.

On some level, I identified this story with Grandpa's death, and fantasized playing the concerto with such emotion that it would bring tears to the eyes of everyone in the audience.

The first weeks after returning from Sewanee, I thought the sadness of no longer seeing Neal had faded. But one morning in late August, as I drove to band practice with my friend Beverly, I recognized him through the window of a school bus. I caught my breath sharply, yearning to see him again. We spoke soon after at the first youth orchestra rehearsal, and it seemed we were not going to resign ourselves merely to being friends.

Neal called me several times at home for long conversations, and a few weeks into the school year, he told me he'd ask his parents to take him to our football game that weekend. With Beverly and two other girls, my senior year I was one of four majorettes who marched and twirled our batons in front of the Shades Valley High School band during the halftime show. I sat at the end of the majorette row in the stands that night, and Neal put his arm around me against the chilly air. I welcomed this physical contact, its comfort and sensuality. I could hardly believe I had a boyfriend who put his arm around me at a football game. Beverly and her boyfriend took Neal and me to my family's house where I introduced Neal to my parents and changed out of my majorette uniform. Then we all went out for cokes and fries.

Neal called occasionally and we saw each other monthly at youth orchestra rehearsals and concerts. In one phone conversation in December, however, Neal gently tried to tell me he was interested in another girl, Amelie. Later I cried because of the similarity of my first name, Emilie, to hers.

Near Christmas I began feeling tired and listless, and needed so much sleep that it alarmed my mother. Wanting to save on heating oil, my father lowered the thermostat to 55° every night around 9:30, and it got colder and colder as I tried to study after dinner. I kept pushing myself to work harder, but by February, I was ill again with recurring sore throats. Needing more and more sleep, I was falling behind in school: I could barely hold my head up in class. My mother took me to a doctor, who ran blood tests and found that symptoms of mononucleosis, including a constant low-grade fever, had recurred. Over that school year, I missed twenty-one days.

I struggled to get all of my homework done as well as my practice time on the piano and oboe, but it soon became clear that I would not have the time or energy to perfect the Beethoven G major piano concerto I had wanted to play in a competition sponsored by the Birmingham Orchestra. The winning student was given the soloist's role in a full orchestral performance, and this was a major competition for teenagers from all over the state.

Neal had stopped calling me in January, and I mourned that loss as well as the loss of the concerto. The band director arranged the first movement of the Mendelssohn G minor, which I had played before, and featured me playing it on the final band concert of the year, but this was small consolation for not being able to play the Beethoven.

On top of mononucleosis and my parents' more frequent disagreements, there was also conflict about where I should go to college. My parents, alumni of the University of Texas, wanted me to attend there, but in a typical act of adolescent rebellion, I refused to apply to the school they preferred.

There were many pressures on the seniors, of course. For me, there were advanced placement English class, marching band and majorette practice during the fall semester, concert band practice and performances during the spring, a full course load of advanced classes, the self-chosen discipline of the concerto – and my unhappy parents and their drinking.

One night, sick and exhausted, I was in tears, missing Neal and wishing I could have played the Beethoven, while my parents were drinking even more than usual. My father started taunting me by singing – to the tune of *There is a Tavern in the Town* – the words, "I feel so sorry for myself, for myself." I fled to my bedroom and slammed the door, but he followed me, stood outside and kept singing: "I feel so sorry for myself..."

2. TRAUMA

Psychological trauma is the unique individual experience of an event or enduring conditions, in which:

The individual's ability to integrate his/her emotional experience is overwhelmed, or

The individual experiences (subjectively) a threat to life, bodily integrity, or sanity.

Thus, a traumatic event or situation creates psychological trauma when it overwhelms the individual's ability to cope, and leaves that person fearing death, annihilation, mutilation, or psychosis. The individual may feel emotionally, cognitively, and physically overwhelmed. The circumstances of the event commonly include abuse of power, betrayal of trust, entrapment, helplessness, pain, confusion, and/or loss.[9]

– Esther Giller

As high school graduation drew near, the atmosphere at home became even more laden with anger and unspoken hurts. Some twenty years later I learned my mother had once again been considering divorce.

After I had refused to apply to the University of Texas as my parents wished, I applied to other schools. I was not admitted to Radcliffe or Oberlin – somewhat outlandish choices for a teenager from Alabama. I decided to go to the University of Michigan, where Dad had earned his PhD in biochemistry and Mother her MA in Spanish. Mother encouraged me to pledge a sorority, recalling how much she had enjoyed it during her college years, but the idea had little appeal.

Except for the usual advice to rest, sleep, and eat healthy foods, the doctor who diagnosed mononucleosis could offer nothing that could restore my energy.

"I think she's depressed," my mother said.

"That's a possibility," the doctor replied, "but the most important thing right now is to eat properly and get lots of sleep."

Always feeling sleepy and sick with sore throats, fever and stopped up ears, pushing myself to study and practice more, trying to prepare for final exams and the annual piano recital – all against the background of my parents' increased drinking and the taut atmosphere at home. This was my life the last semester of high school.

One morning toward the end of the school year, I opened my eyes to a large spider just inches from my face. Still half asleep, I screamed in fear, and without thinking, grabbed a book from the bedside table and killed it. When my mother came in, I told her what happened. Barely recovered from my fright, I scooped up its tangled remains with a piece of paper and showed it to her. "Don't be ridiculous," she said, "it was just a spider."

When final grades were released, Mother was not happy with my C in trigonometry, the only grade below B I had ever received. I told her that missing two key problems on the final had caused the low semester grade, but Mother didn't accept my explanation. At the time I imagined that she read the low grade as a warning I wouldn't manage well at college, but I soon discovered she saw it as something far more ominous.

She made an appointment for me with Harold Larkin, the psychiatrist who had prescribed antidepressants for my dad.

At first, Larkin did not seem that different from any other doctor. His immaculately combed brown hair and black horn-rimmed glasses projected a certain scientific seriousness, but as the appointment progressed, his smile seemed too rehearsed, his voice too studied. I began to mistrust him.

A few days later Mother took me to see a psychologist who administered the MMPI (Minnesota Multiphasic Personality Inventory)[10] and a few other paper and pencil tests. At the second appointment with Larkin, I was asked to sign a standard consent form. It did not state, and no one told me, exactly what I was consenting to. The form I signed stated only that I was agreeing to have Larkin treat me, but nothing about what that treatment might be. There was certainly no mention of how long any treatment regimen would last.

I was suspicious of the entire process, although this, apparently, was typical of psychiatric practice in 1965. Larkin had his own suspicions and voiced them in his notes: "Pt acts in paranoid way. Doesn't want her thoughts changed. Left refusing Rx. Discredits the drug – and refusing to shake hands."[11]

As I found years later in the medical records, Mother had spoken with Larkin while I sat in the waiting room. She mentioned my mononucleosis that spring and also complained that she herself felt "worn out." Her difficult menopause gave her trouble sleeping, and she had been angry with my dad that winter and wanted to divorce him, recalling how he "got upset after I had breast surgery."

Mother reported my excessive need for sleep, my decreasing willingness to help around the house beginning at age fourteen, and my moodiness: "one day full of enthusiasm, next day down." Her version of the spider encounter was that I had had a hysterical reaction. In my mother's eyes, then, normal adolescent behavior and a momentary scare from sharing my pillow with a spider were definite signs of pathology.[12]

Larkin's answer to the psychological problems he diagnosed was electroshock and heavy medication: my entire summer was filled with shocks and drugs. By my eighteenth birthday in mid-July, I had already been subjected to nine treatments. This birthday meant nothing: in 1960s Alabama, the age of majority for decisions concerning medical treatment was twenty-one.

According its proponents, electroshock jolts people out of deep depression, catatonia, or other severe psychotic states; however, there is no agreement among the medical establishment how it might work. One theory put forward by electroshock advocates is that the grand mal convulsion resulting from the electrical current corrects a neurochemical imbalance in the brain.[13]

The original rationale for using induced convulsions to treat psychosis was based on the false premise that epileptics did not become psychotic. Inducing seizures, the reasoning went, should make psychotics less psychotic and more like epileptics.[14]

A more realistic view, held by psychiatrist Peter Breggin and others, is that the calmness sometimes observed immediately after electroshock and the euphoric mood that follows a day or so later are the result of brain damage.[15] While the euphoria is transient, other effects of the treatment, of brain damage, can be permanent. I do not remember ever feeling the least bit euphoric; the only emotions I remember after the treatments were exhaustion, anger, and fear.

Hard evidence for brain damage from electroshock was reported as early as 1952 when Hans Hartelius noted "scattered cell death and small hemorrhages" in the brains of laboratory animals after "relatively small doses of shock." Through microscope examination of the brains of animals that had received shock as well as a control group that had not, Hartelius was easily able to tell from the cellular changes which ones had received the shocks.[16]

These physical changes may contribute to the increasing fear of EST many patients feel during a course of electroshock treatments; perhaps the fear increases because their bodies, if not their minds, are reacting to the cumulative brain damage. By the mid-1950s, Ugo Cerletti, the inventor of electroshock, noted this rising fear: "The patient is not able to explain but it disturbs him at times to the point of refusing to continue the treatment."[17]

Apologists for electroshock now argue that while EST was commonly used as a first-line treatment for depression in the 1950s and 1960s, today it is only indicated when antidepressant medication and psychotherapy have failed.[18] Patient accounts, however, do not agree with this assessment, and often relate chilling incidents of coercion or force. One aspect of the use of EST that has remained stable for more than fifty years is that significantly more women than men are shocked.[19]

A treatment consists, then as now, of premedication with Atropine, a drug to minimize breathing and heart rhythm problems, the injection of sodium pentathol anesthetic, the quick injection of a paralyzing drug to prevent broken bones,[20] the application of electrodes to the forehead, the flow of electric current, the resulting convulsion, and a short period in which the doctor closely monitors the patient's breathing and pulse. Soon afterwards the patient returns to consciousness.

Since no one told me any of this, I had no idea what to expect. I was not even told I was going to have electroshock. I have no memory at all of the first treatment beyond its horror.

Sixteen times during the summer of 1965 Larkin shocked me at his outpatient office in the Medical Arts Building in the Five Points South area. Larkin's waiting room looked like any medical office, and so did the examining room, except for the small microwave-sized box with its dials and electrodes. It began to feel each time as if I were going to Larkin's office to be put to death.

During the third treatment, Larkin did not inject enough sodium pentathol to render me unconscious, but the curare-like drug that prevents broken bones during seizures had completely paralyzed me.

I see him bending over me with the electrodes. Paralyzed, I have no way to let him know I am still awake; I can't even blink my eyes. I feel someone put something rubber in my mouth. Suddenly my entire body wrenches as a heavy blow annihilates me. I develop an ever growing fear of each treatment. Each time, afraid there will not be enough anesthetic, I raise my arms to ward off the shock as long as I can to show Larkin I am still awake.

As Mother drove me to each treatment, a cold sense of dread grew with every traffic light. She always tried to park at a metered space on the street rather than in the parking garage, commenting brightly on her luck if she was able to park more cheaply. I sat rigidly in the seat beside her, trying to keep myself from panicking or expressing my anger at her for what they were doing to me.

In the elevator I would stand very still, fearing what was to come. I would sit in the waiting room beside my mother, hoping no one noticed me until I heard the nurse announce in her cheerful voice, "Miss Hoeffler."

After each treatment I felt drugged and sleepy from the pentathol (a barbiturate) and the succinylcholine (the short-term paralyzing agent) and once home, I would sleep for several hours.

The prescription drugs I was directed to take daily soon visited their side effects: excessive sleep and rapid weight gain. By the time I left for Michigan, my clothes were tight from a gain of twenty-five pounds, and I felt more and more lethargic.[21]

The treatment where I was fully awake but paralyzed left me furious. I told my mother what had happened: Larkin had never had me weighed and did not use enough anesthetic.

The next week a scale appeared in the waiting room, and I was weighed before each treatment. I assumed Mother had called Larkin's office and complained. Hearing the nurse record the number of pounds at each appointment added to my vulnerability and shame about my weight.

Larkin, however, wrote in his notes at my last treatment, "Doing well mother says to go school and get [price of] Rx there."

In a letter to the Mental Health Clinic at the University of Michigan, Larkin wrote:

Dear Dr. Schaeffer:

Miss Hoeffler has been under treatment since June the 8th 1965 for symptoms of depression and a decrease in school function, along with degeneration of social abilities. It was decided to treat her with electroshock, and she has had a total of fifteen treatments.[22] After her 7th treatment she showed remarkable improvement, and by her thirteenth treatment, which was administered on July the 23rd, she herself began to feel a great deal better.

It is my opinion that she will be able to operate satisfactorily in school this fall. She has little if any memory or thought defect from treatment. I would suggest that she have Stelazine in 2 mg size doses twice a day; and that she have electrical treatment every two weeks for a month, then one a month for two months. If she continues to remain entirely asymptomatic during that time, I feel that she could continue with nothing except the medication. I would like to see her again when she comes home for holidays either during Thanksgiving or Christmas. I hope that this will be helpful to you and with all best wishes, I am,

Sincerely,

Harold P. Larkin

Larkin recast my exhaustion from mononucleosis as "symptoms of depression" and the C in trigonometry as "a decrease in school function." And he couldn't have been more wrong about any "remarkable improvement." Although I remembered many details about the treatments that summer, the brutality of electroshock had left me with the aftereffects of major trauma.[23]

Since I had never been away from home on my own before, a large Midwestern university at age eighteen was an utterly new experience, challenging and exhilarating at the same time. I made friends with two girls in my English class, who introduced me to William Butler Yeats and other poets. (Advanced placement English in Birmingham paid off; I placed out of freshman English and began my English courses at the sophomore level.) And I had fun on a few dates with a red-headed history major named Walter.

I lived on the top floor of a large low-rise dormitory. Looking out my window one rainy day, I saw an almost solid layer of different colored umbrellas moving across the quad. My own umbrella was a bright yellow, which made me think of sunshine even when it rained. Watching the umbrellas below, I felt excited being in college, imagining how my own umbrella looked when I crossed the quad.

I dutifully checked in with Dr. Gould, the psychiatrist I was referred to by the student health center. He surprised me by telling me I obviously didn't need electroshock treatments, and at a second appointment, that I really didn't need the psychotropic drugs either. Despite this welcome news, the shock treatments over the summer had instilled so much fear that I was reluctant to see him regularly, afraid that he might still find something wrong with me and have me shocked as Larkin had done.

Since I only saw him two or three times all told, I didn't tell him about the recurring flashback of being shocked while fully awake. Dr. Gould continued Larkin's prescription for Stelazine and added one for Thorazine when I told him how much trouble I had getting to sleep. I didn't like taking the drugs, but if I didn't take them, I was unable to sleep.

Many nights dropping off to sleep I would feel myself falling backward and see Larkin bending over me with the electrodes. My arms would flail upwards as I tried to tell him not to shock me yet, and I would suddenly be wide awake, my heart racing.

I would dream of going to visit a friend in the hospital after surgery, and opening a door at the end of a hall, I would suddenly find myself on a mental ward, mistaken for a patient and not allowed to leave. The shock treatments of the previous summer were over, but for me, they were still happening.

Michigan made me homesick for familiar things, not so much for my parents or Birmingham as the happiness and comfort of Grandma's home in Ballinger: the ranch, the dogs, and even the lemon ice cream. When the Thanksgiving holiday came, the family budget wouldn't allow a flight to Birmingham for such a short trip. The dorm stayed open, but the empty halls were deadly quiet, the wintery campus lonely with so few people there. The cafeterias closed, except one in a different dorm, where all the students still on campus had their Thanksgiving dinner.

A phone call to a different state was much more expensive in those days, and since I didn't want to bother my mother needlessly, I tried not to call home too often. If I finally gave in to my need to speak with her, she would already be in bed. My mother was in no mood for words of comfort. "Don't call," she would respond angrily, "put it in a letter!" Sometimes she merely hung up.

Perhaps it was a mistake to have come to Michigan. So many nights after things quieted down in the dorm, I longed to go home. I began to think I should transfer to the University of Texas, where my parents had wanted me to apply in the first place. That way I could take the bus to Ballinger some weekends and not feel so far from home.

At Christmas I flew back to Birmingham for the holiday. My grades came in the mail: all B's. My parents admonished me to improve my grades the next semester, while the university advisor wanted me to sign up for more hours. I knew I could make all A's and planned to do better when I went back. The holiday was uneventful, and Mother took me to see Larkin on December 28.

Larkin wrote Dr. Gould the next day:

Dear Dr. Gould:

I saw Julia Hoeffler while she was home for Christmas and I think you have done a splendid job with her. I see no indication to suggest that anything should be changed. I believe, in my experience, that continuing the Stelazine indefinitely would be desirable. Since her sleeplessness has responded promptly to the Thorazine that you gave her, I think that she should continue that. The question came up about her courses this year. She is taking three subjects now and plans to take four this coming study period. The counselor at school has suggested that she would need to do that because of the investment that is being made in her by the University. I would suggest that perhaps we wouldn't want to do that. But rather keep it to three the remainder of this year. I am very satisfied with the progress that she has made. She was right sick last summer and we were having a nip and tuck as to [whether] we were going to make it to school, so I think we had better play it conservative. If you agree. Perhaps you might call him if he needs to have that support in cutting this course down to chemistry, math, and German this time. With best wishes, I am, Sincerely,

Harold P. Larkin

This concern over my course load came not from me but from my mother, who had brought it up during the medication check meeting with Larkin. I had wanted to take more courses but Mother felt that might be too demanding.

A forward-thinking school, the University of Michigan deferred rush until the week before the second freshman semester. I had no interest in pledging a sorority, but to please my mother, I had reluctantly agreed to participate.

I felt ambivalent about returning to Michigan. I dreaded the clutching feeling of homesickness, heightened by the recurring nightmares. Yet I also wanted to keep discovering literature with my new friends and get to know Walter better. When I boarded the plane, my mother warned in a stern voice, "If you call home one more time, you're coming home." She meant come home for good.

The early round of rush parties was held in the common rooms of the women's dormitories. Since I didn't really want to join a sorority, I was already somewhat ill at ease maintaining the pretense. Knowing that rushees were being judged as to their suitability for membership only increased my awkwardness.

All from the North or Midwest, the girls seemed pleasant enough, sophisticated and smartly dressed. They politely asked me the usual questions: where I was from and what I was studying. The conversations around me, however, were nothing but mindless chatter about sorority life, fraternity parties, and clothes.

At one of these first parties I happened to look back at the girl who had just introduced me to some of her friends. Chatting with one of her sorority sisters, she was rolling her eyes and making a face. I couldn't stop from thinking she was talking about me. Was it my Southern accent? The weight I had gained from the drugs? Although I knew they had no way of knowing, could they somehow tell I had seen a psychiatrist and had had shock treatments?

Later that night, homesick once again, I needed to talk about my hurt feelings and how the whole process of rush was so hypocritical and shallow. I broke down and called my mother. She had no patience this time. "Pack your bags and get home!" she said, and then hung up.

The idea of withdrawing from the university and packing my bags for Birmingham should have been more stressful than it was, but I mainly felt relief: I was going home. Dropping out of college was much more serious than it is today. The Dean of Women had me sign something that said I would never try to enroll at the University of Michigan again. Since I had excellent SAT scores and reasonable grades, however, a transfer to the University of Texas would be something I could deal with a month or two later.

When I called my mother to give her my flight information, I also wanted to mention my thoughts about transferring. When she answered the phone, I told her when I would arrive. "What?" she asked. There was a moment's silence. She said she would meet me at the airport and we would talk then. She hung up without saying goodbye.

On the plane coming home, I went over my plan once more. Although I had spent several weeks each summer at Grandma's house, I had never been so far away from home by myself in my life. But Grandma was family, and her house felt more like home than my parents' did. I thought I could stay with Grandma one semester, perhaps get a part time job in Ballinger, and transfer to the University of Texas.

I thought we would go home from the airport, have dinner, and talk about my plan. I assumed they would see its logic: since Grandma lived a reasonable bus ride from Austin, I wouldn't be so homesick if I could ride the bus up to see her every few weeks. But I never had the chance to tell them.

When I got off the airplane, Dad met me at the gate and we went downstairs and collected my suitcase. He spoke only a few short words of greeting, and busied himself with the luggage. Mother was waiting in the car with the motor running, and Dad held the door for me to get into the back seat. I wondered for a moment why they had brought the Volkswagen instead of the more comfortable four-door Chevrolet.

As we drove off, neither of my parents spoke more than a few words. When Mother turned a different direction at a familiar intersection, it occurred to me we weren't taking the usual route home. "Where are we going?" I asked. There was no answer. I repeated the question more urgently, but Mother kept her eyes on the road and Dad stared wordlessly straight ahead.

I came to a horrifying realization. "Are we going to a hospital?" I asked. But still, neither of my parents answered. I began to feel strangely numb, much as when I had frozen up as a seven-year-old watching my unfamiliar Grandpa on the porch.

I was trembling, I could not speak well, and I had trouble getting out of the car. We had arrived at the only private mental hospital in the area. It later occurred to me that they must have brought the two-door VW because they thought I might try to escape when I realized we weren't going home.

Mother guided me to the admitting room, and the nurse, a middle-aged woman with a bouffant hairdo and harlequin glasses, held out a form for me to sign. Everything felt as if it were happening in slow motion. I could not make myself sign the form. It would be an act of self-betrayal: I put the pen down but couldn't say a word. "If you don't sign it," Mother threatened, "I will!"

The only dignity left to me was not to scream, cry, or fight back, so I pushed down all the outrage and signed the form. Then I walked away with the nurse, and did not look back. As I left the admissions area, I felt enraged toward my mother but refused to show any emotion.

Years later as a grown woman, I was still proud of not begging or pleading with my mother, but walking away with the nurse and not once looking back at her.

"Is he going to shock me again?" I asked the nurse when we got to my room.

"He's very hard on those who have to have it twice," she replied.

My room was a private one – I later learned every room on the hall was private – with wall-to-wall carpeting and its own bathroom. During my entire stay, I don't recall seeing any grown women except the nurses, only girls around my own age. Except for the decorative bars on the windows, the ward felt like the dormitory at Michigan, only much nicer.

The morning of the second day, the nurse woke me up early and handed me a cup of coffee. I've never liked coffee, so I left the cup on the bedside table, turned over and went back to sleep. When someone woke me by rolling me onto my back, I had no idea what was happening. I saw Larkin and the shock machine and panicked.

After this first shock treatment, the nurse reported "quiet day, cooperative, wanting to go home." That evening, however, I became angry at my imprisonment. The nurse wrote, "Pt hostile, belligerent and wanting to go home. Wanting to talk to the Dr." I remember feeling angry and protesting, demanding that they let me go home. And I remember quite well what happened next – I was pushed to the floor and held down while the nurse gave me an injection. The shot seemed magical: the drug worked almost instantly and I remember my amazement at how suddenly I felt peaceful and sleepy. According to the notes, "Taractan 50 mg i.m. [intra muscular]" was the drug used, and soon afterwards the nurse recorded that I was asleep.

For the first couple of weeks, I stubbornly kept telling the doctors that I had cleared my return with my parents before I left Michigan and that I had a plan to alleviate my homesickness at college. They dismissed my account as "irrelevant material used as an attempt to explain her present situation."

I was kept at the private mental hospital for five weeks. The alternative was the state hospital – Bryce – where it was rumored that lobotomies were still performed. I was shocked fifteen times during the thirty-six days I was in the hospital; added to the sixteen treatments from the previous summer, the total now rose to thirty-one.

At the time, there was no psychotherapy or group therapy at this hospital as there was in other parts of the country, only occupational therapy. OT, such as it was, consisted of games like shuffleboard, group singing, jigsaw puzzles, and other activities in which the inmates were expected to participate. Nurses reported daily on each patient's activities with brief written comments. From my records, typical entries were things like "attended afternoon piano concert," or "bingo, table tennis." The doctors used these reports to determine whether patients were improving. After the first six shock treatments, given every other day from January 24 through February 1, my "progress notes" recorded that I was "improving" and "beginning to be more sociable."

One of the doctor's notes went into more detail: "Julia Hoeffler is much more cooperative than she has been in the past … She is becoming pleasant, cooperative, and recently gave a piano concert for the other patients, which I understand was quite good." At the daily piano session one of the nurses asked me if I would play, and I obliged with sections of the Mendelssohn concerto I still remembered. The stormy opening was a way to express my anger.

This duly noted improvement came not from the damaging shock treatments but from an accidental meeting in the hall. One afternoon as I stood in the door to my room, I saw a nurse leading a group of young women patients down the hall. A teenager no older than I stopped and said to me in a bright voice, "Are you going to OT today?" Drugged and shocked into a stupor, I had no memory or understanding of what OT was, but the dark-haired girl lowered her voice: "They like it if you go," she said.

The idea slowly registered that if *they* liked something, it would be a good idea to do it, and I followed the group to OT. The friendly girl helped me participate in the occupational therapy of the day, and soon the nurses were noting such items as "Julia attended evening movie" or "participated in table tennis."

A few hours after each electroshock, one of the doctors would "visit" me, as they termed it, and talk to me in my room to ascertain the effect of the earlier shock treatment. The early reports, initialed by various psychiatrists, were negative, such as this one from January 18: "She is receiving EST but stays in the bed most of the time. All day yesterday she was in bed and slept 10 hours last night. She has shown no interest at all in activities thus far." And this one from January 20: "Spends all her time in her room. She is very uncooperative. Does not mingle with others."

By January 25, there was some note of progress, "She had EST yesterday morning with good results, grand mal convulsion.[24] She still spends a great deal of time in her room, but adapting to the hospital a little better the past few days. She has shown a minimal interest in occupational, recreational and social activity. Becoming interested in leathercraft, going to the daily piano playing, attended the song session. She was also seen working in a group on a picture puzzle and doing some reading."

My reaction to being abducted and then disbelieved when I told the doctors my parents had ordered me to come home was entirely understandable – anyone would have resisted this abusive treatment. And the amount of drugs, combined with those used to administer the electroshocks and the effects of the shocks themselves, did not make cooperation easy. I was still protesting – asking, crying, or begging to go home well into the second week of my five-week stay.

This stubborn persistence was a trait that actually helped preserve my sanity in spite of Larkin's false diagnosis, yet both he and my mother interpreted it as one more symptom. "Bullheaded behavior part of the illness," Larkin wrote in a hospital note. Since neither my mother nor Larkin would listen to reason, in order to maintain my own integrity, I had to try to adopt the role of a docile, submissive patient to convince them I had accepted his diagnosis. This was extremely difficult to do, since it meant I had to mask my outrage at the injustice of my hospitalization.

As I realized the advantage in pleasing the doctors by co-operating and socializing with the other girls on the ward, the doctors noted more improvement. Once I told one of the nurses I thought I would do better if Larkin would stop shocking me. The next day I was subjected to an extra treatment, so I knew not to mention it again.

❋

Although I kept telling the doctors I had cleared my return with my parents before I left Michigan, they didn't believe me. Much later, I realized my mother simply had no memory of the phone call I made the night after the rush party. She drank every night and took barbiturates to sleep, and I had called late, after she would have taken her pills. She was also taking a tranquillizer at the time, as she reported in a hospital interview:

January 15, 1966.

Social Worker interviewed Mrs. Hoeffler who was extremely talkative and anxious and apparently completely unable to control her feelings, her emotions or her conversation. The interview lasted approximately an hour, during which Mrs. Hoeffler relived almost her entire life history with her husband, who it sounds, is an extremely ill man, ... although he does manage to carry on with his job at the University Hospital as a PhD in biochemistry. Apparently Dr. Hoeffler has said on numerous occasions that he has seen his own problems in the patient. Although he has seen Dr. Larkin, it has not helped him very much and Dr. Larkin feels that there is no point in treating Dr. Hoeffler any further. Mrs. Hoeffler also appears to be in need of help, although she is not as severely ill as her husband. She is on tranquillizers, apparently at the moment on Mellaril but seems to manage to cope with her environment and the situation which to all intents and purposes has not been an easy one.

Because my mother didn't remember the phone call, much less that she had ordered me to come home, when I called and said I was on the way, she thought I had made the decision to return to Birmingham on my own, out of the blue. And this is how she remembered it.

"When Julia tried to start the second semester," Mother wrote years later to a friend, "she was so confused and upset she packed up and came home instead, and that was why she had to be hospitalized in 1966." Of course this was also what she had told the doctor and he believed my mother, not me.

I kept protesting that the shock treatments were hurting me, but it did no good. Any show of strong emotion, any criticism of the doctors could lead to extra shock treatments.

I fell back on the prayer I had prayed as a young child after Grandpa died, just to comfort myself the only way I could. The final, most important petition of my prayer, "And please let me get to kiss and hug Grandpa Miller one more time," led to fantasies of Grandpa coming to rescue me. He would have brought his guns and made them let me go. Or since he was a lawyer he would have gotten a court order and gotten me out that way. He would have slapped my mother across the face and told her "How dare you do this to my granddaughter!" And he would have slammed Larkin against the wall and threatened him. He would have gotten me out. But he was dead, and all I had was the prayer.

As I learned to conform outwardly to the doctors' expectations, they gave me a pass to leave the hospital for lunch with my mother or go home to spend one night on a weekend. Each time I was scheduled for one of these outings, however, I was subjected to a shock treatment a few hours prior, as if the doctors wanted to ensure I was subdued, docile, and drugged.

I didn't know I was to be discharged until the very last night. My parents had known for some time, but had resisted the idea, having thought my hospitalization would continue into March, as noted in another interview:

Spoke to Dr. and Mrs. Hoeffler for a lengthy period of time... The main purpose of the interview was to discuss post-hospital plans for Julia. It was decided that she would enroll as a student at the Birmingham-Southern College for the next quarter, which begins on March 21... Although they would have liked her to have gone to a college which has a bit more prestige. Apparently Birmingham-Southern [is] prepared to take the patient, all things being equal, and if they have a satisfactory report from Dr. Larkin and from the matron at Ann Arbor University where the patient stayed.

The parents were also concerned about who would care for patient when she came out of the hospital, and although I have discussed this with Mrs. Hoeffler on a previous occasion, the question was again brought up whether she should ask her mother to come from Texas. I emphasized that the patient on discharge from hospital could not be left alone, and it was therefore most important that arrangements be made for her post-hospital care. Mrs. Hoeffler said that her mother would be prepared to come and prior to the patient getting ill, she always got on well with her maternal grandmother. Dr. and Mrs. Hoeffler seemed to have accepted the fact that the patient was going to be in the hospital for, they feel, about six weeks, and every time they are told that she will be out before March, they seem unable to accept it.

The day before I was discharged, Larkin interviewed me in his office. His most pressing question was whether I had attained a certain insight: "You must have known that if you came home like that, your parents would put you in the hospital, didn't you?" he asked, looking at me closely, his head cocked to one side. "Yes," I replied, "I should have known." Yet underneath, I felt heartsick to answer this way, since I had thought no such thing.

It is impossible to convey the cat and mouse dynamic just beneath the surface of this conversation. Larkin – the man who had hurt me over and over and who had blasted me into unconsciousness with an electrical surge when I was paralyzed and utterly powerless to resist – this man was now quizzing me, trying to seem casual, reasonable, trying to get me to be "reasonable" too, and agree that I should have known my parents would force me into a mental hospital if I came home from college.

And I knew he was on the lookout for anything I might say that would reinforce his definition of me, anything that might indicate a need for more shocks or stronger drugs. I knew what the truth was; I saw the situation clearly. But he had the power to destroy me and there was no way to convince him or anyone else that I did not need this kind of treatment, that I was not crazy. If I protested that I was not mentally ill, Larkin would see it as a symptom of mental illness and conclude the treatment had not worked.[25] I had no choice but to agree.

The morning of my discharge there was an unscheduled shock treatment. Because of the danger of patients throwing up and inhaling the vomit, they were never submitted to a treatment after eating breakfast. I had learned quickly that if a breakfast tray was brought to my room, I was safe from a treatment that morning. But this morning was different.

When Larkin and the two nurses burst in with the shock machine, I pointed to the breakfast tray and said, "You can't shock me, I've eaten breakfast."

"That doesn't matter," Larkin replied. I looked frantically at one of the nurses for some sign of compassion or support, but she only averted her eyes. And I was subjected to one last shock before my discharge, again, most likely to render me drugged and docile before I went home.

As I stood at the top of the concrete steps waiting for my mother to bring the car around, I looked up at the building and spotted the window of my room on the third floor. I vowed that I would never forget what they had done to me. And I vowed that I would never betray myself by believing what they wanted me to believe: that I was in any way mentally ill. I was finally going home, and as far as I knew, there would be no more treatments. Yet it was important to me to remember that what they had done to me these past five weeks and the summer before was wrong.

Compared to accounts of others subjected to EST, the amount of memory loss I experienced was small. Although fairly large chunks of my memory were erased – I have no memory whatsoever of where I was when Kennedy was shot and only fragmentary memories of high school – I did retain clear memories from my five weeks in the mental hospital, as well as a general sense of the chronology. Perhaps my unusually light memory loss in comparison to others' accounts might be that the smaller amount or different wave form of electricity used in EST in the 1960s may have caused less brain damage.[26]

It also may be that my ability, unconsciously and consciously, to suppress my anger fooled Larkin and the other doctors into believing my condition had "improved" before their shock machines could damage my brain even more than they did.

At one point Larkin wrote in a letter to another psychiatrist: "She has in the past been encouraged to give expression to her thoughts and these unfortunately have frequently been varying degrees of psychotic. This coupled with the fact that she has been bright and a good student has resulted in our being deceived on more than one occasion as to the quality of her thought."

Now, writing in 2014, I am glad Larkin and the other doctors were "deceived."

3. ... AND MORE TRAUMA

A man devoid of hope and conscious of being so
has ceased to belong to the future.[27]

– Albert Camus

I had assumed that Larkin's releasing me from the hospital would signal an end to the shock treatments, but he had enlisted my mother to monitor me and report to him on my mood and behavior. I remained on "maintenance" electroshocks for over three years.

My mother's role as monitor slowly became clear to me. In the spring of 1966, she sometimes held the treatments over me like a threat. "We can't afford a nice private hospital next time," she said. "Next time we'll have to send you to Bryce."

One day the two of us were driving somewhere in the car. The dogwoods were just beginning to bloom; their intense white flowers stood out in explosive bursts against the dark wood of the other trees. I was sitting quietly, looking out of the window, even feeling somewhat peaceful seeing the budding dogwoods. "You're depressed again," Mother said, "You need another treatment." "No, Mother," I said, "I'm just enjoying looking at the dogwoods."

I begged my mother several times to stop the shock treatments and let me talk to a psychologist. "The insurance pays 80% for Dr. Larkin and only 50% for a psychologist," she would say with unassailable firmness. "Besides, psychologists always say it's all the mother's fault."

Larkin and my parents had pulled strings and gotten me accepted at Birmingham Southern College, but the dormitory had no more spaces for the 1966 spring quarter. So I lived at home and commuted to college in a car my mother bought for me a month after I was released from the hospital.

The day I went to campus to have my picture taken for my student ID, I remember standing in front of my bedroom mirror, my face swollen, my eyes puffy and red. Today I have only a photocopy of that picture from a college transcript. A young woman's bloated, expressionless face stares out at me through the photocopy's grey streaks, and I think of the fog of medications through which I saw the world.

The many drugs made the half-hour commute to the college seem like negotiating a complicated maze. At first I couldn't re-member the route from one day to the next. Coordinating the gearshift and clutch, staying aware of traffic, remembering to watch for a traffic light to turn green before a horn jolted me to action – all became tasks demanding my full attention. In class I had trouble following lectures, my drugged body demanding that I go home and sleep.

My mother was not happy with my progress. A social worker's interview that same spring noted: "Mrs. Hoeffler is very concern-ed about Julia as she was refused admission to the dormitory of the college, and although Julia has not shown much disappoint-ment, Mrs. Hoeffler feels this has been a major letdown as Julia has refused to socialize very much with the other college students. Mrs. Hoeffler is also concerned about Julia's weight. She has no enthusiasm to lose weight and spasmodically goes on a diet."

That summer Mother and I drove to Texas and attended sum-mer school together at the Austin campus. She had thought we would share a room in the graduate student dormitory, but the housing officials wouldn't allow it. All of the freshman women's dorms were full, and I was put into The Contessa, a private dorm, with meals and full maid service.

My roommate, Frances, was a lovely young woman who told me she had been given one shock treatment as a younger teen. But their family doctor had told her parents that she was merely having "growing pains" and advised them to stop the shock treat-ments. Frances had never been subjected to another. I was excited, thinking her story might convince my mother to make Larkin stop shocking me, but when I tried to tell her, Mother refused to consider the idea.

Our time in Austin meant we had to drive back to Birmingham for me to receive a shock treatment. During the 700-mile drive, I had to sit quietly while Mother made superficially encouraging remarks on what good progress we were making or how many miles we had covered. I became quieter and quieter, responding as little as possible, knowing that if I expressed my fear or outrage she would report it to the doctors.

My fear of the treatment grew mile by mile, remark by remark, but somehow my unconscious self, as if cooperating with my trapped state, caused me to grow increasingly unresponsive to the fear and anger. Aware of the overwhelming emotions, yet unable to fight back, unable to escape, I simply became frozen.[28]

Years later I wrote in a letter to a friend: "I don't think I will ever go to hell, but I think I know what hell is like, and that is close to what hell is like, having to sit there for 700 miles, going to be shocked, and having to cooperate because I had no choice, and because I could not convince my mother that the shock treatments were hurting me and that all I needed was someone to talk to, to be treated with respect, and for my parents to quit drinking and to try to treat each other and me with respect."

We arrived in Birmingham late that night, having made the trip in one long drive. After just a few hours of sleep, I sat up in bed the next morning and swung my legs over the side, still groggy, knowing I would soon have to face another shock. Out of the corner of my eye I saw a large black spider slowly crawling across the sheet where I had just been sleeping. I felt nothing, had no reaction other than picking up a book from the stand and smashing the spider. I picked it up with a tissue and threw it into the wastebasket. In some deeper place I dimly sensed I could not scream and risk the repercussions of any strong show of emotion, but my conscious mind registered only the mechanical impulse to kill the creature.

Beginning in the 1966 fall quarter at Birmingham Southern, I lived in the dormitory and came home on the weekends. One

Sunday evening my dad, as usual, was getting more and more drunk as the evening wore on. At the dinner table, he began his typical teasing and I made my usual mistake of talking back to defend myself. He was particularly obnoxious that evening, and since I had been taught never to tell anyone to "shut up," I demanded, "Hold your tongue!" His reply was to grasp his tongue and attempt to say, "But I can't talk when I hold my tongue." Drunk herself, Mother sat observing this juvenile interaction keenly, her eyes narrowed.

The next morning she called Larkin's office and made an appointment for me to be shocked the following day.

After a regularly scheduled treatment, hearing the date read out at the receptionist's desk would set in motion a numbing process of which I was only slightly aware. Knowing the date of the next treatment signaled this process to occur in the days prior to each shock, but it could not occur before an unscheduled one. Larkin wrote in his note from this extra treatment, "She has slipped some this last 2 weeks and needs come now in 3 weeks. Mother says Father and daughter give friction if she not well."

Reading psychological studies on abuse and trauma in the 1980s, I realized that what had happened was an unconscious process of dissociation, a numbing of my dread of the upcoming treatment.[29] Dissociation encompasses a broad continuum, beginning with casual daydreams, through simple detachment while anticipating a painful experience, to the complete removal of oneself from a traumatic event as it is occurring – watching oneself from the ceiling or experiencing something completely different in a location far away.

My experiences were of the simpler kind, similar to how I froze when watching Grandpa on the porch. Yet just beneath the numbness, panic threatened to erupt. This was probably one reason I walked very slowly and sat as still as I could in the waiting room before an outpatient shock treatment: I must have been afraid that any extraneous movement would allow the terror to break through.

The next few days in the dormitory, I was outraged at my mother for not listening, for punishing me with an extra shock treatment, merely because I had verbally defended myself against my drunk, belligerent father. I decided to fight back the only way I could: by not going home on the weekends. If I were not there, my father would not have the opportunity for drunken comments. The drugs I was prescribed and dutifully took helped suppress my anger and sadness.

I still could not break from my parents either financially or emotionally. Even if I could have mustered the nerve to run away, where would I have gone? What would I have done? I had never had a job and didn't even have a social security number. I had no money other than my weekly allowance. I could not have imagined turning to prostitution. If I had been caught and taken back to my parents, they probably would have had me formally committed – it did not take much to do that in 1969 – and I would never have gotten out. Since I was a diagnosed mental patient, for all I knew the police would have come looking for me.

People in situations of abuse, particularly children, often seem illogically attached to their families. They keep loving them, keep returning to them, and I was no exception. By now I was damaged and trapped, and I had no one else.

I kept hoping they might listen, that they might understand and take me to another doctor for a second opinion, or I might find a doctor or psychologist I could talk to, someone who would listen and understand that I was not mentally ill, not insane, had never had anything remotely resembling a hallucination and that I was being damaged more and more by the drugs and shocks. I kept thinking that if my parents could stop drinking they would stop being opponents and start being parents. If they would treat each other and me with respect, they would understand that I was not crazy, and they would see the harm the shocks and drugs were doing to their daughter.

The drugs I was prescribed – Thorazine, Stelazine, Compazine, Artane, and others – took their toll in many ways. Beyond making it difficult to concentrate and study, the drugs sedated me so much that I often fell asleep in class and had so little energy that every walk across campus was an ordeal.

Thorazine and other drugs of its class are now called "dirty" or "promiscuous" drugs because they act on many different receptors in the body, causing multiple side effects.[30] What I knew at the time was that the drugs caused me to feel extremely sedated and to keep gaining weight. A recognized and common side effect of these drugs, this weight gain was interpreted by both my parents and Larkin as a lack of self-control and one more symptom of psychosis.

It seemed to me at the time that Mother wished I had never existed. On one shopping trip to the mall, when I was embarrassed and ashamed at trying on clothes because I had gained more weight, she remarked angrily, "I don't know why I had to be saddled with you." I did not answer, but stood there, silently trying to block the pain.

The strange deadening process always began several days prior to each shock, and I dimly realized that this helped me survive. If I fought back, cried, or complained, the shocks would be increased in frequency. I was not conscious of doing anything to initiate this deadening, but I was vaguely aware of my robot-like, emotionless state that increased up to the day of a shock.

Since my discharge from the hospital, the outpatient shocks were no longer at Larkin's office in Five Points South, but in a building near the hospital housing the doctors' offices and outpatient services. Once a mansion or a country club, its enormous main floor had a double curved staircase to the doctors' offices on the second floor.

When I was taken for a shock, we first checked in at a receptionist's desk on the west side of the main floor. About ten minutes after swallowing the Atropine pre-medication, a nurse called my name. I would walk with her to the east side of the main floor and then alone down a narrow enclosed winding staircase. I would stare at its rubber treads as I made my way to a cold basement room with one small window high on the whitewashed wall.

A small wooden chair, a table with a couple of magazines, and a radio tuned to an easy listening station were the only furnishings. The rest of the room and a door leading to another hallway were obscured by a white curtain. Sitting in the chair alone, waiting to be shocked, I felt no conscious fear of what was about to be done to me, yet I also knew, somehow, that I was blocking an underlying terror of being destroyed. Trying to run away or fight back would only bring more shocks and stronger drugs, so the deadening of my mind and emotions was my only protection.

When they were ready to shock me, I would hear footsteps as Larkin and the nurse came down the hall and through the door behind the curtain. Then the nurse would pull back the curtain, revealing a gurney set up with the electroshock machine on a small stand next to the pillow. I was to remove any jewelry or hairpins and lie down.

Always, I was afraid that Larkin would not give me enough anesthetic and I would be paralyzed but unable to tell him I was awake, so at the last minute, I kept my arms raised as long as I could. After the shock, the nurse wheeled the gurney through a long hallway in the basement to the west end of the building to a small recovery room where the patient regained consciousness.

A nurse sat outside the door of the small cubicle and when she heard me stirring would come in and make sure I did not fall trying to get off of the gurney to get dressed. Then the nurse would lead me up another enclosed spiral staircase on the west side of the building, the twin of the one which I had descended. This opened into the waiting room where my mother would be sitting in one of the white plastic chairs. I would then walk with her over to the appointment desk to schedule the next treatment.

The outpatient treatments were scheduled so no patient waiting for electroshock would see or hear another patient undergoing the procedure. As I sat at the small table waiting for one treatment, however, I heard someone gasping for breath behind the curtain. As Larkin hurried to turn on the oxygen, he brushed against the curtain, pulling it back slightly, and I saw a man on the gurney with a plastic mask on his face. The nurse was forcing oxygen into his lungs, squeezing a hand pump for every breath. In my blank, dissociated state, I felt nothing, but I never forgot what I saw. After he had been wheeled away, they came back with an empty gurney and I climbed on for my own shock treatment.

Although I was able to lie down and submit to the treatments at the outpatient unit, back in the dormitory I often felt deep anger at what my parents and the doctors were doing to me.

Late one night in the girls' dorm at Birmingham Southern, a group of us were in our pajamas, talking in the lounge. Linda, another outpatient at the hospital, began telling us about her treatments. She had pleaded frantically with the doctors, she told the hushed group, and resisted the treatments tearfully but in vain. Yet the nurses would comfort her before she lay down on the gurney.

Linda acted as if she had fully accepted the doctors' definition of her and even relished the role of mental patient. I couldn't understand why she wasn't angry about what was being done to her. Accepting the doctors' label was something I would never do, and Linda's dramatizing a shock treatment for her friends appalled me.

One night I walked into Peggy's dorm room – she was a girl I had known since grade school. "If they don't stop doing this to me," I blurted out, "I'm going to kill myself!" Peggy, whose older brother had committed suicide when she was thirteen, took me at my word. She told me later that she had said to herself, "I cannot let this happen." She wasn't too happy with her current roommate and asked me the next day, "Julia, would you like to be room-mates?" After consulting the dorm mother and getting approval, we were moved into the same room.

Over the two years we roomed together, Peggy helped me in many ways. She got me involved with the theater group by taking me to the plays and persuading me to sign up to help with props and later to hold book for the director. When we had early classes together and, drugged with all the tranquilizers, I would otherwise have slept through any alarm clock, Peggy helped me wake up and get to class. She also talked to me about what was being done to me and asked me questions about Larkin. Peggy was concerned that Larkin never talked with me. All sessions I had with Larkin were either shock treatments or ten-minute medication checks with my mother always present.

Another note from the hospital records concerned a spaghetti supper I attended at a Presbyterian church near campus. The minister spoke with us as a group afterwards, and he seemed so understanding, so approachable, that I wanted to talk to him individually. I mentioned this to my mother, and she must have discussed it with Larkin, for in the records he noted, "Preacher OK but he 2 understand 1ˢᵗ." Larkin would have spoken with the minister and cautioned him that I was mentally ill if I had pursued my wish to talk with him.

The next summer, during a trip to Texas with my father, I worked up the nerve to ask him some questions about Larkin. I felt less afraid of being made to have an extra treatment for asking questions because I had just had a treatment before we left Birmingham, and we were several hundred miles away from Larkin on our way to visit Dad's parents for their fiftieth wedding anniversary.

"How can Larkin tell if I am getting better if he never talks to me?" I asked.

Dad replied, "Do you know that sodium pentathol can be used as a truth serum?"

"Yes, I know," I said, having seen enough television shows to know something about it. Dad said that sometimes before or after a shock treatment Larkin gave me an additional dose of pentathol so that I did not remember being questioned. Since I could not lie under the truth serum, Larkin would know for certain what I felt or thought.[31]

By the fall of 1968, Larkin had decreased the frequency of the treatments to once every twelve weeks, and my body had longer to recover in between shocks, although the fear of the procedure never left me. Several times I argued with my mother.

"There was never anything wrong with me," I would tell her. "I'm 'getting better' because the shock treatments are less frequent."

"No," she would counter, "The shock treatments are less frequent because you are getting better."

In October, my dad won a door prize, a black Labrador puppy, at a meeting of the Izaac Walton League, a conservationist group. Isabella – named for his having won her on Columbus Day – was an exciting, affectionate presence in an otherwise dismal household. She was a beautiful animal, curious about everything, and friendly to everyone. I enjoyed being around her, since I had always wanted a dog. But the main task of caring for Isabella fell to my mother, since Dad was at work for long hours each day and I was away at the dormitory most of the time, at least during the week.

One Friday afternoon I came home to my parents' house for the weekend and was looking forward to taking Isabella for a walk, but I could not find the puppy. I asked my mother where Isabella was, and she replied, "I let her out. She has to learn to stay out of the street sometime." I looked for Isabella and called for her in the yard, but the woods around our house were fairly dense and eventually I gave up trying to find her.

The house was at the top of a hill and trucks speeding around the curve had sometimes hit our mailbox. So it was no great surprise when about an hour later someone rang the doorbell and asked if we owned a black Labrador puppy. Isabella had been killed by a car. We went down the driveway with a cardboard box to retrieve the body.

Mother was in a hurry to get the body to the vet – she had called him and asked what to do – because she didn't want Dad to come home and be "upset." So I loaded the box on some newspapers on the floor in front of the back seat. Mother already had the engine running. As I was walking around to get in on the passenger side, Mother said through the window, "Poor Isabella. Couldn't learn to stay out of the street."

"Isabella is dead," I kept thinking as Mother drove to the vet's office. "Why aren't we crying?" That evening Mother told Dad about it in a casual way over their usual drinks; he barely reacted. They never mentioned her again. It was as if Isabella had never existed.

One Friday night in November I found myself alone in the dormitory. Mother and Dad were driving to a bridge tournament in South Carolina. They hadn't made a hotel reservation, but were planning to drive until they were tired and get a room somewhere along the way. There was no way I could get in touch with them.

My roommate Peggy had gone out with her fiancé, Michael, and was not going to return until very late. The dormitory was deserted. All of the other young women had gone out to a sorority function or a college dance. I was alone on the third floor.

I was desperate for someone to understand how what they were doing to me with the shocks and drugs was damaging me, killing me. I tried to call my parents, thinking that if I tried just one more time they might listen to me, but of course they had already left town. I called the bridge club where Mother played, thinking that someone there might know where they were staying overnight, that maybe they had mentioned something. But I had to be careful not to sound too emotional, because they might tell Mother, and she would then make me have another extra shock treatment.

I called my friend Jim, another student from the theater group, but he wasn't home and there was no way to leave a message. I couldn't call Peggy because I didn't know a number for where she might be. I was afraid to call anyone else because I couldn't risk anyone knowing how I felt. Mother had threatened me with extra shock treatments when I had cried before.

I was without hope. At that time I had never been told any details of my diagnosis or treatment, and as far as I knew the treatments would continue the rest of my life. I had no means of making anyone believe me or listen to me about what I knew to be true. The only way I could escape a life of continuing shock treatments, I began to think, was death. Death was the only way I had to make them stop hurting me.

I thought about how to do it so I couldn't be rescued or revived. I could take a whole bottle of Thorazine or some of the other drugs but figured that if anyone found me, I would be taken to the hospital, my stomach would be pumped, and then they would increase the shocks and send me to Bryce because I had attempted suicide. So I knew it had to work. It couldn't just be an attempt. But I didn't have a gun, and I didn't want to cut my wrists in the bathroom and risk anyone finding me before I was dead.

As I thought about taking my own life, time slowed down, and I experienced a sort of narrowed, tunnel vision. The light was that strange, flat half-light either side of sunset.

Then I remembered that when my brother had been about seven, he had chipped a tooth on the bottom of the swimming pool because he had dived into the shallow end. The doctor had told him that he was lucky, that he could have broken his neck and died or been paralyzed completely if he had hit his head on the bottom at a different angle. And I realized that one way I could succeed at killing myself and make them stop hurting me was to jump head first off of the fire escape at the end of the hall.

Our room was on the top floor, the third, but the dormitory was built on the side of a hill, and the ground was almost a story lower than a typical third floor. I reasoned that if I jumped off of the fire escape head first, I would hit the concrete of the parking lot and break my neck and die. I hated my parents for hurting me. I wanted to make them stop hurting me.[32]

Time slowed down even more. My senses were heightened, and I heard a diffuse roaring sound around me. I decided to do it. I was just about to get up out of the chair; if I had stood up, I would have walked down the hall and jumped off the fire escape.

Just then the telephone rang. It was Jim. He had just arrived home and wanted to check with me about the rehearsal time for the college theater group the next day.

I burst into such severe sobbing that I almost choked. Jim was alarmed. He had always been kind to me but didn't know what the doctor and my parents were doing to me. "I don't think you should be alone right now," he said, slowly and carefully. "Connie [his wife] and I are going to go see a movie, and I am going to come over there and get you. I want you to go downstairs to the living room and wait for me. Don't stop to do anything. Just go straight downstairs and wait for me. I'll be there in five minutes."

The three of us went to see a movie: *Rachel, Rachel.* Exhausted and numb, I couldn't follow what was happening on the screen. But in the dark movie theater, I could sit quietly without having to explain what had happened or answer anyone's helpful questions. After the movie, Jim and his wife took me back to the dormitory where, with the aid of Larkin's prescriptions, I fell asleep.

Larkin's truth serum technique with sodium pentathol either was apparently not used or didn't work at the next treatment. He had no inkling of my suicidal intent, for the only note he recorded was "Doing very well [return in] 14 wks."

During the entire time they shocked me, June 1965–March 1969, no one told me if they would ever stop the treatments. As far as I knew, they would have kept shocking me forever. Peggy kept after me, telling me to get my mother to take me to a different doctor to get a second opinion. But my mother would never have considered it, even though she knew that Dr. Gould, the psychiatrist at Ann Arbor whom Larkin had recommended, had told me I did not need those medications, much less the shock treatments. The only option I knew was to keep silent and not fight back.

Peggy was engaged to Michael, who was in law school at the time. After he looked up the legal aspects, she told me, "You are twenty-one years old now and they can't do this to you any longer on the strength of your signature at eighteen." I mentioned this to my mother a few times, but nothing came of it, and I was afraid to push it much further out of fear of more shocks. I didn't know that in order to invoke my legal right, I would have had to state to Larkin directly that I did not want any more shock treatments. By this time, I was so traumatized and afraid of the shocks and Larkin

I would probably not have had the nerve to stand up for myself even if I had known it was my right to do so.

Because I had been shocked and forced into a mental hospital, I thought no one would ever want to marry me. So when Sean, a boy I had dated briefly in high school, came home for spring break and wanted to go to bed with me, I figured this would be the only chance I would ever have to find out what sex was like. It was 1969, and the sexual revolution was in full swing. Many of the young women in the dorms were sleeping with their boyfriends. My parents were out of town, and Sean and I went to their house for our affair.

My period was two weeks late, and I had to work up the courage to tell my mother. "So, you never had sex with Neal that summer at music camp after all, did you?" she said. "Your father thought you had, I thought you hadn't. I was right. Well, don't worry about it. Worrying about your period being late can make it late. And besides, you have a treatment coming up and maybe that will take care of it."

"But Mother," I replied, "my next treatment isn't until April! They said April!"

Mother went straight to the telephone and called Larkin's office to change the date of the treatment. Since she was leaving that Saturday to direct a bridge tournament, my dad would take me to the hospital. He had never taken me for a treatment before; my mother would never schedule one if she knew she was going out of town. I felt helpless terror at having to face yet another unscheduled electroshock.

4. Escape and Rescue Operations

The opposite of cruelty is not kindness;
the opposite of cruelty is freedom.[33]

–Philip Hallie

Mother must have told Dad that I thought I might be pregnant. The Saturday morning after she left for the bridge tournament, Dad told me to get all of the medications I had been prescribed. He seemed very determined – angry, but controlled, and somehow for once I could tell the anger was not directed at me. The pill bottles, five clear plastic cylinders containing all the drugs Larkin had prescribed at one time or another, half filled the small paper sack he got from the kitchen.

When I woke up from this treatment – sooner than usual – I was angry. I began doggedly trying to get over the rails and climb down off the gurney so I could get my clothes from the table next to the bed. The nurse hurried into the room and tried to persuade me to lie back down. When I kept trying to get off the gurney, she gave up and helped me by lowering the rails and steadying me as I stood and reached for my clothes.

In the car after the treatment, I was still foggy and under the influence of the various drugs from the IV. Before Dad started the car, he gripped the steering wheel firmly with both hands and said, "The doctor says you don't have to have any more treatments."

Still groggy, I asked, "What?"

And he repeated himself, slowly and significantly. "The doctor says you don't have to have any more treatments."

"Oh," I said, without emotion. But I remember thinking that now that I felt almost dead and might never recover, it didn't much matter if they shocked me anymore or not.

To this day I do not know why my father acted as he did that morning, but I will always be grateful that he intervened.

No one ever mentioned it again. Mother never said anything about their having stopped shocking me, and neither of my parents spoke of how they had whisked me from the airport directly to the hospital. I was too afraid to bring it up in case they might decide to start the shocks again. Nothing in the records suggests why Larkin stopped the treatments.

Concerning this final treatment, however, Larkin wrote "MAY BE P.G," in caps, underlined in heavy ink. And there were many notes to the nurse about different medications. Each note was similar and said something like *"Medication name.* Who prescribed this medication and when?" The answers were all the same: "Dr. Larkin prescribed this medication in *month, year.*" I was taken off of several of the medications and told to keep taking Thorazine, Stelazine, and Compazine, and Larkin added a new drug, Norpramin. As the weeks went by, I discovered I was not pregnant, so that fear receded.

At the end of the spring term, I transferred to the University of Alabama, in Tuscaloosa, and, no longer subjected to shocks, was able to make good grades again. I made several friends, among them two girls who were sisters and roommates, Irini and Despina Chris, two of my closest friends today. I was glad to have a car now, because most weekends I drove Irini and Despina home and then went to my parents' house to do my laundry. Saturday afternoon I was back at Irini's and Despina's and spent the night with them.

The next morning I would go to church with the family at the Greek Orthodox Cathedral. I was awed by the beautiful life-sized icons painted on the iconostasis (the tall screen between the altar area and the rest of the church), the mysterious smell of incense, and the reverent tones of the Greek chant and hymns. Irini and Despina showed me how to light a candle for a prayer before the service and explained the Greek liturgy. After church we'd drive back to their house for a delightful Sunday dinner – Mr. Chris had been a chef and had owned his own restaurant. I was entranced with these beautiful friends who enjoyed sitting around the dinner table talking happily and relishing each other's company.

Larkin only saw me for brief appointments, with my mother always present. He never talked to me about anything other than what medications I was taking, so he knew nothing about my new friends.

Reading the records more than twenty years later, I was not surprised that he had attributed my "improvement" that summer solely to the new drug he prescribed. "Norpramin," he wrote, "got rid of all depression mouth dry sleep all nite … continue this med." In another note, a doctor standing in for Larkin at one medication check, wrote, "Julia Hoeffler doing well best I've ever seen her Making A's at Univ Norpramine [sic] did the trick."

As I became closer to Irini and Despina, I entrusted more of my story to them, telling them about my parents' drinking, the conflict at home, and the treatments. Irini later told me she'd asked her father how this could happen to someone. "There is not a thing wrong with Julia," Mr. Chris said. "She just needs to be loved."

Mother worried that I might wear out my welcome at my friends' home. "If Julia is bothering you," Mother told Irini in a phone call, "I'll see that she doesn't come around anymore." "Oh no, Mrs. Hoeffler," Irini answered, "we love Jules and love to have her here."

My friends' generous hospitality was rooted in their heritage as well as their religious tradition. *Filoxenia*, as Despina later told me, was the ideal of being "friend to the stranger," related to the biblical story of Sarah and Abraham and the visit of the three angels, depicted in the icon of hospitality painted prominently on one of the arches below the dome of the Birmingham cathedral. As my friendship with the two girls flourished, they and their parents became a second family to me, a beautiful and healthy one.

Irini also told me about a conversation she had with my mother during a visit to campus. "Irini," she said, "I want you to do something for me. When Julia talks about majoring in math I want you to encourage her and when she talks about majoring in English or music, I want you to discourage her." In spite of her

58

traditional Greek upbringing with its emphasis on honoring and obeying parents, Irini, a loyal friend, did the very opposite.

I discovered that the University Health Center offered free counseling to any enrolled student, and I was still determined to find someone to talk to. I told my mother that she could not object because the counseling sessions were free.

I went to the counseling center, where I met the graduate student who was to be my counselor, a young man working on his master's degree in psychology. At the end of the session he asked me in a curiously loaded tone, "So, how did you like the West Coast?" I had no idea why he would ask such a question, and quickly went through my mental rolodex, remembering that I had visited the West Coast with family when I was four, and also that I had visited a friend near San Francisco when I was about fourteen, but I did not mention either of these trips.

The man's tone made me wary. "Oh, it was OK, I guess," I said. After that one visit to the health center, still suspicious after the man's question, I did not return. It was only in 1988, when I received the hospital records through an attorney, that I understood why this fellow asked me about the West Coast.

From the hospital records, I learned that my mother had called Larkin and told him I was going to go to the counseling center. Larkin then wrote the head of the center a letter that contained some interesting misinformation:

Dear Dr. Dinoff:

I have seen Julia Hoeffler off and on over a period of the past four years. She began with an acute psychosis that was not recognized until the last year of high school, and we were able to bring it under control during the summer months, only to have her go away to school and a psychiatrist at the school clinic took her off her medicine. She sold her books, bought an oboe and ran away to the West Coast. Her parents got her back, brought her back into treatment and after that initial experience we have been able to successfully manage her illness. She had had her last (fiftieth)[34] electroshock treatment in March of 1969. She is continuing on

Norpramin 25 mg q.i.d, Stelazine 2 mg q 12 h. and Thorazine 50 mg at hour of sleep. She must continue on these medications and if she should require consultation in regard to their management between the time that she has appointments here, I would want to know about it.

Larkin had either confused me with another patient, mis-interpreted something my mother had told him, or simply embellished his story with dramatic details, perhaps to bring home his point more strongly that I should keep taking the drugs he had prescribed. I had had no need to buy an oboe, since my parents had given me one for Christmas in 1963. I had never sold my books – even in 1988 I still owned several books I had used at the University of Michigan. And even Mother could swear that I had never "run away to the West Coast."

A few weeks before I graduated from the University of Ala-bama, Dad missed the last step going down the basement stairs and fell. He shouted up to us, and mother opened the door.

"I've broken my arm!" he cried out.

"You didn't break your arm," Mother called down to him, somewhat irritated, as if she really didn't want to be bothered.

"Madam, I made the highest grade in anatomy at medical school and I have broken my arm!"

"All right, we'll call the doctor," she answered.

My mother's lack of empathy in this exchange was character-istic. Whether it was her daughter's homesickness, her husband's fear she might have breast cancer, or the pain of a broken arm, her own crushing need left her only a narrow space to connect to the emotions of others. She could not tolerate her own strong emotions, much less accept those expressed by others.

Graduation day in Tuscaloosa was sunny and bright. To honor my achievement, Dad, a professor in the medical school, marched in the faculty procession in his University of Michigan PhD regalia. In a photograph Mother took, the white cast on his right arm stands out sharply against the blue of his robe, while the two of us, father and daughter, stand in front of the president's mansion, smiling in the hot sun.

With a BS degree in math and a minor in French, in August 1971 I was accepted into the graduate program in French. I was offered a scholarship, but Mother persuaded me to decline it and attend the Honeywell Institute in Atlanta so that I would be more likely to get a job. I completed a three-month computer programming course and began to look for jobs in the computer industry, such as it was in 1972. Sending out resumés and scouring the newspaper ads for jobs, I had little luck.

One afternoon late that winter, I was lying on my parents' bed reading – there was an excellent reading light on top of the headboard. Dad was at work, and Mother was in the den, watching TV, playing solitaire on a TV tray, and sipping a martini.

I needed a tissue, so I started looking for the box. It wasn't on the nightstand, so I opened the sliding door of the headboard to look for it. There, on Mother's side, was a stack of about seven issues of the magazine *Psychology Today*.

About three years before, at Birmingham Southern, the professor in my psychology class offered to get the students a group subscription to this new magazine at a special rate. I had liked the magazine so much I decided to continue my subscription after the class was over.

While I was at school in Tuscaloosa, I had the magazine sent to my parents' address since I came home to Birmingham almost every weekend. "Mom, has my magazine, *Psychology Today,* been sent here?" I would ask. "Have you seen it in the mail?" Mother always told me she hadn't seen it and once suggested that perhaps the subscription had run out. So I had more or less forgotten about it. Yet here was this stack of magazines, all addressed to me. My mother had been intercepting them in the mail and hiding them.

I was angry at my mother and went into the den to confront her. She made a strange face she often made, pursing her lips while shrugging her shoulders. She didn't deny hiding the magazines; in fact, she said nothing at all.

"Well, they're my magazines," I said. "I paid for them out of my own allowance, and I am going to read them." I stomped off to my bedroom where I read all afternoon, every single magazine.

There were several articles about how emotional problems were caused by abuse or misunderstandings in the family. And the portraits of the families where these things happened were similar to my own. No wonder my mother had hidden the magazines from me!

It all seemed totally reasonable. This was my problem, not anything biological. My supposed problem was actually caused by family dynamics of verbal abuse. And suddenly, I had an odd thought: "This magazine will be the key to my getting over what they did to me." I always remembered this strange thought. Later, I came to believe that it must have come from God in some way.

Soon after this, I was offered two jobs. One was in Birmingham at the Southern Research Institute, where my father knew some of the scientists and had heard of an opening in the computer department. The other was a job as a maintenance computer programmer in Houston. I flew there for the interview, was hired, and moved to Houston in April 1972. I stayed for a couple of weeks with friends of my parents until I found an apartment and rented some furniture.

The new job brought challenging days and the opportunity to master new computer languages and contexts. But the nights were always troubled. I had difficulty sleeping, often waking several times a night with nightmares about the shock treatments. Almost every night I re-experienced the feeling of falling backwards and would awaken suddenly, my arms flailing up to ward off Larkin and the shock.

I was still taking Thorazine, Stelazine, Norpramin, and Compazine, and began seeing a psychiatrist Larkin had recommended in Houston. I had constant sore throats, but nothing specific was diagnosed when I first consulted a Houston internist recommended by a co-worker. A large part of my fatigue and ill health must have been from chronic lack of sleep. And living in Houston was difficult: the first time I had ever lived away from my family for any length of time other than the one semester at Michigan.

One afternoon about three months after I started my job in Houston, I came home from work and checked my mailbox. Inside was an issue of *Psychology Today*. I had renewed the subscription after I discovered my mother's having hidden them, and had kept subscribing to the magazine after I moved to Houston. I had even considered dropping the subscription because the magazine wasn't as interesting as it once had been, but I still renewed it, specifically because I remembered the thought, "This magazine will be the key to my getting over what they did to me."

I read the entire magazine that afternoon, front to back. There were some interesting articles about group therapy and encounter groups where everyone was honest about their feelings to each other. This sounded heavenly to me, and I was impressed with the possibility of honest communication. I knew intuitively that what had been wrong in my family was the lack of that very thing.

For some reason, that afternoon I even read the classified ads in the back of the magazine, something I had never done before. One ad was for a center for human potential in Houston that hosted an open house every Thursday.

The next week, I drove to the address, which was on a quiet residential street in the Montrose area. About seven people attended, and sitting on big comfortable cushions on the floor, we watched a couple of films about people doing Gestalt empty chair exercises and T'ai Chi. The psychologist who ran the institute spoke for a few minutes about the institute, its purpose, and the different kinds of groups offered.

After the talk, he invited everyone for a cup of tea in the dining room. Stacked on a sideboard were boxes of Celestial Seasonings herbal teas, something I had never heard of. To a young woman from Alabama, everything seemed very "cool and California."

I struck up a conversation with the psychologist's wife, a calm woman with long brown hair, who helped me serve myself some tea. I expressed my enthusiasm about the place. Remembering how the ad in *Psychology Today* was supposed to be "the key," I asked her if she knew a psychotherapist she might recommend for someone like me who had had electroshock treatments and was looking for a psychologist to help get over them.

The woman was a bit put off by my request, it seemed. "The institute is a center for human potential and growth," she said, "not for therapy, and we do not normally give out names of therapists. I do have the name of someone who might be able to help you, but you have to understand that we are a growth center and we do not normally give out names of therapists."

"You mean, if I promise never to tell anyone you gave me the name," I asked, "you'll give me this man's name?"

"No," the woman repeated, visibly irritated. "You have to understand that this is a growth center and that we do not normally give out names of therapists."

I was about to repeat my objection, but I realized the important thing was to get the man's name, and I didn't want to annoy the woman further. "O.K. I understand," I said. "Can you tell me his name?"

And the woman gave me the name and phone number of Paul Tobias.

I met with Paul weekly for about two years in the early evening after work. His greying hair and warm brown eyes spoke of experience and intelligence, but most important to me was his calm reassuring voice. Paul listened to me and helped me understand that what had been done to me was not my fault. He put me in touch with a psychiatrist who helped me withdraw gradually from all the damaging drugs Larkin had prescribed. And Paul referred me to Dr. Collins, a general practitioner, who discovered I needed supplementation for a thyroid condition.

It is difficult to describe what happens in psychotherapy: there are setbacks and breakthroughs, and sometimes it seems that there is no progress. Some of the sessions with Paul were painful, but I knew Paul was helping me and that he cared for me. It was beautiful to be able to trust someone again and to know Paul would not hurt me.

64

Early on, Paul asked me how I had come to be in Houston, so far from Birmingham, and I told him about the two job offers. "I don't know why I accepted this job and not the one at home," I wondered. "Survival!" Paul replied, "You wanted to survive."

One evening in a session a couple of weeks later, I had been crying and then began to speak – one word at a time, agonizingly, as if the words were being wrenched from me. Even as I said one word, I did not know what the next was going to be. One by one the words came out: "God … damn … and … fuck … it … I … have … a … right!" I sat there, exhausted by having said these few words. "Yes, Julia," Paul replied, "you have a right to be loved."

During the two years I worked with Paul, I also attended several groups offered at the institute. All of the groups were facilitated well, and I learned much about honest communication and relationships.

In the spring of 1973 I was happy to be working with Paul and withdrawing from the drugs. I invited my mother and Irini to come for a visit during their spring break. Both of them were teaching in Birmingham.

I was so delighted to have found Paul that I wanted Irini and my mother to meet him and come to a session with me. I told them about this plan soon after their arrival. That night Mother said casually, "Irini, I need to get some things from the grocery store, come on with me." They came back shortly with some groceries and we made dinner.

Later that evening, Irini came into the bedroom and told me she had to leave early, that she couldn't stay long enough to go meet Paul. I begged her to stay, but Irini just said she had to go. Mother had already called the airline company and made arrangements for Irini's flight to be changed to the earlier date, and my friend left for Birmingham.

I was both puzzled and sad at the time, but what actually happened only became clear later that summer. Irini told me over the phone that my mother had driven to the grocery store, parked the car, and broken down sitting in the driver's seat, pounding the steering wheel and saying over and over, "He's going to say it's all my fault! He's going to say it's all my fault!" Collecting herself somewhat, she told Irini that I had told her that I didn't want Irini to stay and meet Paul, but that I didn't want Irini to know this. So, Irini would have to tell me that she had to leave early but not let me know that she knew I wanted her to leave.

I was astounded – Mother had flat out lied to Irini, and then persuaded Irini to tell me a lie to cover up her own. The only reason I can imagine was that Mother didn't want Irini there in case she decided to strong arm me into coming home to Birmingham for more "treatment" at the hands of Larkin.

Oddly enough, two months later Irini called to tell me that she had learned through the mother of one of her high school students, a nurse at the hospital, that Larkin had been dismissed from the hospital for indiscriminate use of electroshock.

1973 was a year of much argument about the inhumane treatment of patients in mental hospitals. Although the famous anti-electroshock movie, *One Flew Over the Cuckoo's Nest*, was not released until two years later,[35] 1973 saw the publication in the journal *Science* of David Rosenhan's article, "On Being Sane in Insane Places."[36] Rosenhan and a number of others voluntarily signed into different mental hospitals, claiming to hear voices say innocuous words like "Thud." All were diagnosed with mental disease, usually schizophrenia, even though soon after being admitted as patients, they reported that they no longer heard any voices, and throughout their hospitalizations acted completely rational. They were eventually released, with "schizophrenia, in remission" listed in their discharge notes.

Probably after Larkin was fired, later in 1973 or 1974, one Birmingham psychiatrist acted as a whistle blower, resigning in protest over the excessive use of electroshock at the hospital where Larkin practiced. He appeared on a local television talk show to discuss his resignation.[37] My parents must have known something about this, and my father subscribed to and regularly read *Science*, so he would have seen the Rosenhan article. But neither of my parents mentioned any of this to me.

❀

By the spring of 1974 I reached the decision to quit working as a computer programmer and go back to college to study English or music. I had gotten a job working in a bookstore and had saved enough of my salary to cover tuition at the University of Houston. This was a dramatic move toward independence: to do something I wanted to do rather than what was expected of me. I didn't tell my parents, and my mother, coming out for one of her visits, learned of it only after I had handed in my resignation.

"How could you throw away such a cushy job?" Mother asked angrily. "Do you want to be a ward of the state?" She insisted on going with me to see Dr. Douglas, the psychiatrist recommended by Paul who was helping me withdraw from the last of the psychotropic drugs originally prescribed by Larkin.

Mother stood in front of the doctor's desk. "This child needs some medication," she said in her most authoritarian schoolteacher tone. Cowed as usual by my mother's anger, I sat passively watching the scene. Dr. Douglas wasn't yet forty, and my mother, aged fifty-seven, rising to her full height, overpowered him as well. Obediently taking out his prescription pad, he wrote two prescriptions, one for Vivactal, an antidepressant to be taken in the mornings, and one for Serentil, a tranquilizer for bedtime.[38] I took the drugs for the remaining few days of my mother's visit, but the side effects were so pronounced I refused to take them anymore.

Later that summer my mother did try to understand. "I knew you were not happy at that big company," she wrote. "Perhaps this time around in college you will get some of the things you missed out on the first time."

5. The Catching Up Years

Most of all that love has found us, Thanks be to God!

– Harvest Hymn

In 1974 when I went back to college at the University of Houston, I had to choose between majoring in English or music. After carefully reading the college catalogue, I realized that it would be impossible to complete a degree in music as quickly as in English, since music courses were all sequenced and English courses could be doubled up. I regretted the choice, but well aware of the practical issues of cost and time, knew I could not do both.

I met with the chair of the English department, who on the strength of my GRE scores tried to recruit me as a graduate student right away. But I was hesitant to jump in so quickly and decided to take English courses as a post-baccalaureate.

From this point on, I pursued catching up with a vengeance. I knew that at age twenty-seven I had to work hard to reach the point I might have been had I been able to attend college as a regular student, not being shocked and drugged.

I moved into a co-op in October, and accepted a work study position at the help desk in the computer center, helping students correct their job control language so that they could run their assigned computer programs. This was where I met Tom Welton, a computer science major commuting from Galveston.

When my car broke down, Tom gave me rides to and from the university for several days. He liked the co-op where I was living and shared a few meals with us. He came with me to a poetry reading in Houston's Montrose area and heard me read at the microphone. Soon we were in love, and we drove down to Galveston for me to meet his father. By January 1975 we had moved in together in an older apartment across from the Hermann Park Rose Garden. As we settled into the new semester, we decided to get engaged.

My mother met Tom when she came out to Houston to stay with me during a tonsillectomy advised by Dr. Collins because of recurring throat infections. After we removed any evidence that he was living with me from our apartment, Tom stayed at our friend Karl's place. Mother was impressed with Tom and how affectionate he was, sitting by the hospital bed, petting my hair, and giving me ice chips. "You grab that one. Marry him!" she said when Tom left the room. "If your father had ever been so affectionate with me..." I also took Tom to meet Paul, in a sense for a father's blessing.

Tom and I both wanted to marry in a church, and we joined Christ the King Lutheran in Rice Village. During the last weeks of our pre-marriage counseling sessions with Pastor Peterman, a drunk driver jumped the median and collided with our car. I was injured with a kind of sideways whiplash. I was not wearing a seatbelt, something I always regretted afterwards. At the emergency room, they removed pieces of glass from my face and assessed my injuries. Tom was driving, and emerged relatively unharmed, since he had used his seatbelt.

A couple of weeks after the accident, we rushed again to emergency room for an extreme muscle spasm that had cut off the circulation to my right hand. I was in considerable pain, and was prescribed muscle relaxants to calm the spasms.

The night before our last counseling session with Pastor Peterman, something strange happened. It was in the form of a dream, but I knew that it was much more than a dream.

I no longer prayed my childhood prayer about seeing Grandpa Miller again, but I was always aware of losing him, even twenty-two years later, and set to be married to Tom in a few weeks.

In the dream I was in the den of Grandma's house. There was a giant greyish white presence in the corner. There was that intoxicating, earthy, clean smell when it is hot and dry and a rain is badly needed and it finally starts to rain. I was afraid and awed, knowing I was in the presence of something miraculous and holy.

The towering greyish-white figure across the room started communicating with me, mind to mind. I realized it was Grandpa, and he told me that he had come back to give me a message. He told me that they didn't normally let anyone come back this late and that he was almost ready to go on up. But he got special permission because he loved me so much and wanted to give me this message. He told me I should stop missing him and wanting to be with him. That I had Tom now and that Tom would be my husband soon and would take care of me, and that I should concentrate on Tom and stop wanting to be with Grandpa.

And then the most miraculous thing of all happened. He leaned over and picked me up, as if I were five years old again, and he swooped me up to his face and kissed me, and I felt the stubble on his cheek against my face.

I woke up, terrified and ecstatic at the same time. I shook Tom awake, told him the dream and cried a long time. The next day we went to see Pastor Peterman, and I told him the dream too. "I don't know what you think," I said, "but I don't think it was just a dream. It was in the form of a dream, but I think it was more than a dream. I think it was Grandpa coming to give me the exact message he gave me." And Pastor Peterman said he thought that was true, too. He said that as a pastor he had heard many people's experiences and that this was not strange to him.

This was, of course, the answer to my prayer: the prayer I had prayed as a small child grieving the loss of my beloved Grandpa and again as a frightened teenager locked up in a mental ward with bars on the windows and being shocked over and over by sadistic doctors. God had let Grandpa come back and kiss and hug me one more time, just as I had prayed. I do not know how much the prescribed muscle relaxants may have contributed to the dream, just as I am aware it could be interpreted as simple wish fulfillment, but I believe there was something more.

Tom and I were married in May of 1976, at Christ the King on a joyously bright and sunny Sunday afternoon – not in a park, as in a 1970 popular song I remembered, "What are you doin' Sunday?"[39] Irini and Despina came from Birmingham to be bridal attendants, and after consulting a Greek Orthodox priest, Pastor

Peterman incorporated the ritual of the *stephana,* crowns for the bride and groom, from the Greek marriage rite. Irini held the crowns as Pastor blessed them and then placed them on our heads.

Just for fun, I arranged for our friend Karl to change into a rented gorilla suit for the reception in the church fellowship hall, and Irini and Despina led the Greek dancing. Irini and I had taught Tom some Greek dance steps, and Tom, the gorilla, and I danced in a line as the guests applauded.

Later that year, Karl and I were having lunch at Alfred's Deli in Rice Village, not far from the Texas Medical Center. Looking up from our conversation, I noticed a man entering the restaurant, who then sat down in a booth several yards away. I was certain it was Harold Larkin. My impulse was to confront the man but I was too afraid and just wanted to get away from him. I convinced Karl we should leave as quickly as possible. Later Karl told me that he was struck by how the color had completely drained from my face the moment I saw the man come in and by how shaken I was for several hours after the incident.

In the summer of 1979 or 1980 Irini and her husband visited us in Houston. Irini told me something remarkable: she had read an article in the Birmingham newspaper that said that Harold Larkin had been disciplined by the State Board of Medical Examiners. I wrote to the board after Irini's visit and requested that they examine Larkin's medical practice, stating that I felt that his treatment of me had been malpractice. I was too afraid, and too ashamed because of the stigma of what had happened, to go into detail. The board responded with a letter asking for more details, and also stating flatly: "Harold Larkin does not practice medicine in the state of Alabama."

I didn't pursue this information further, being so far away from Birmingham, and also so caught up in catching up, as it were. Yet in the back of my mind I resolved someday to find the article.

These were happy years of accomplishments, learning, and just being young adults. I taught English as a teaching fellow and discovered I enjoyed heading a classroom and doing research for graduate seminars. During the last two years of my graduate work in English, I started studying piano privately, which awakened my desire to continue serious music study.

Weekly lessons brought regular and longer practice time on the piano, and soon I was working on Chopin nocturnes, Bach preludes and fugues, and of course more Beethoven. One night Tom, still awake after I had dozed off, noticed my fingers moving rapidly on the pillow. He woke me up and asked if I were dreaming I was playing the piano. Sure enough, I had been hearing the music, seeing the printed score, and feeling the piano keys as I dreamed I was practicing a Bach fugue.

With Tom's support and encouragement, I continued my studies, completing a master's in English literature in 1981, a bachelor's in piano performance in 1983, and a master's in performance in 1986. Tom went to work for a large computer company and finished his BS in computer science. I taught piano in a preparatory school of music while completing my music degrees.

Dark memories still troubled me. Sometimes during the day while doing something routine – washing dishes or driving – I would find myself wondering why Mother and Dad took me from the airport without even asking why I had come home. One night I had a nightmare about Larkin and the shocks. My tossing and turning woke Tom up, but as he gently tried to wake me, I was still locked into the dream and thought he was Larkin, about to "treat" me with an electroshock.

I became interested in writings about the Holocaust and kept some of those books in the spare bedroom. Every so often I felt the need to read these accounts, which always made me cry. I wondered then why I needed to read this material and indulge in such bouts of crying. Only much later did I see that this was a means of grieving vicariously for what had happened to me.

One study I read later suggests that when trauma survivors seek out intensely dramatic books or films, they are unconsciously attempting to master their original trauma in a situation of lowered risk.[40] Knowing that I could close the book or turn off the television allowed me some measure of control.

For the most part, these years served Tom and me well as we established our relationship on a firm footing and achieved success in work and education.

In the spring of 1986 I decided to pursue music study further, and applied to several PhD programs in musicology, a good way, I decided, to combine my love of both literature and music. So, in the summer of 1986, Tom and I prepared to move to Austin for me to begin the PhD program in historical musicology at the University of Texas, where I had been awarded both a fellowship and teaching assistantship. This, I thought, would be the last round of catching up and I could then begin an academic career.

6. FALLING APART ...

The wounded surgeon plies the steel
That questions the distempered part;
Beneath the bleeding hands we feel
The sharp compassion of the healer's art
Resolving the enigma of the fever chart.
— T.S. Eliot, *Four Quartets*

The move to Austin went well, with Mother helping in the search for a rental house and even in the packing and moving. She was getting older now, but she gamely carried small items to the car or into the newly rented house in spite of the pain from her arthritis. During the week, Tom would have to stay in Houston for work, so we rented a small apartment for him close to the office.

One problem was unsettling. I had been having increasing menstrual pain, and after a D&C in the fall of 1985 knew that I had a growing fibroid. After consulting several doctors, all of whom recommended surgery, Tom and I decided it was best for me to have the operation with Dr. Leeds, who had been my gynecologist for seventeen years in Houston. The plan was to schedule the surgery over Christmas holidays so I could continue the graduate program without a break when the new semester began in Austin in mid-January.

The first semester was difficult, but no more so than other academic programs had been. I only saw Tom on the weekends when he would drive the 200 miles up from Houston. But I carried on in my graduate courses, even though I had trouble sleeping and still had nightmares about Larkin and his shocks.

By the end of the semester, the pain had become more severe, and Tom and I prepared for me to have major surgery. I spoke at length with the anesthesiologist, warning him that I feared that a fast induction might trigger a flashback to Larkin standing over me with the electrodes. He agreed to use an extra sedative before the anesthesia and to make the induction as slow as possible.

Mother came out to Houston to help, visiting the hospital every day and helping Tom in the apartment, cooking for him or taking him to dinner. She bought another twin bed for the apartment so I would have a place to sleep for the two weeks after the surgery. She was having problems with her back and brought her own inflatable mattress, which, she had found, was the most comfortable way she could sleep while traveling.

I underwent the surgery without too many complications. A removal of just the fibroid was not possible, and a partial hysterectomy was necessary, along with the removal of the appendix and gall bladder, since I had been having gall bladder symptoms for several months. The phenothiazines Larkin had prescribed for so long are now known to increase the chances of gallstones.[41]

In stark contrast to my hospitalization twenty years earlier, these eight days were mainly a positive experience. The nurses were kind and explained everything well, and Dr. Leeds explained why the hysterectomy and other surgeries needed to be done. Today it's likely that a surgery could easily have removed just the fibroid, but this was not the case in 1986. I recovered for about ten days in Tom's apartment in Houston, and then Mother and I set out for Austin.

We stopped in Giddings for lunch in a Dairy Queen. I was still feeling vulnerable, as if the incision in my stomach would burst open if I did anything too quickly. We sat down in a booth and began to eat lunch.

My mother, perhaps trying to offer some consolation for my now not being able to have children, said, "Well, I never much wanted children. You and your brother just came along and I took care of you." But then she continued, "Just think, if I hadn't had children I wouldn't be here right now. I might be doing something better." I could find no words in reply, but muttered something about needing more napkins and carefully stood up to get some.

Mother stayed in Austin for two more weeks and then flew back to Birmingham. In February Tom and I drove to Houston to see Dr. Leeds for the last post-surgery examination.

"Has your mother gone home?" Dr. Leeds asked casually.

"Yes," I answered.

"Good," he responded. I wondered what he had observed; it wouldn't have been the first time Mother had tried to take charge of my medical treatment.

One night I dreamed that Mother, Dad, and my brother had driven into the driveway of the rental house in Austin. I was watching from the bedroom window above. They got out of the car and stood on the side of the driveway. Enraged they had intruded on me uninvited, I suddenly began to grow and grow, like Alice in Wonderland. I smashed my arm through the window, reached down and knocked my father and brother aside easily, as if they were nesting wooden dolls. Grabbing my mother, I closed my hand and squeezed.

The scene changed and I saw myself from across the street. At 100 feet tall, I had burst through the roof of the house, and fire was flashing out of my eyes, like Godzilla. I raised my hand up to where I could see it better and opened it. Mother had turned into a black rubber disc. Raising it to my mouth, I bit down on it, hard, and woke up terrified.

I realized that this was a memory fragment of EST: the black disc was the bite guard placed in the mouth before the convulsion to protect the tongue.[42]

As the spring semester continued, there were more and more nights of fitful sleep fragmented by nightmares. During the day, I couldn't concentrate: thoughts of the original trauma of Larkin's shocks kept intruding into my daily routine, sometimes ending in bouts of crying when I was alone.

Unexpected sounds I could ignore before began to startle me. During an afternoon seminar, a leaf blower suddenly chugged into action outside, and I involuntarily drew in my breath, looking in alarm in the direction of the sound. One of the other students noticed my strong reaction and asked me what was wrong. Later, working on a complex assignment in the library, I was on edge when a student wearing a jingling charm bracelet kept walking by as she went to check out more recordings from the desk.[43]

Despite my overall positive experience of the surgery, I began to suspect that something about the drugs used, the vulnerability of being hospitalized, or having to interact with my mother during her visit might have caused these disturbing symptoms and memories. [44] I had read about PTSD, post-traumatic stress disorder, among Vietnam veterans, and even though I had not experienced military combat and was not a war survivor, I wondered if what was happening to me was somehow similar. I wished I could talk to Paul about what I was feeling, but he had moved to California in 1975.

I set about searching for a psychotherapist in Austin. This was not an easy task, since Paul was not someone that many people could measure up to in my eyes. I was leery of those who might prejudge me because of Larkin's label. I needed to find someone who understood that I had never been mentally ill, but that my problems stemmed from what had been done to me. In the 1980s PTSD was a condition recognized only as a consequence of wartime experiences or natural disasters, and some of the therapists I interviewed could not understand my need to resolve what had happened to me in the 1960s. [45]

After interviewing many prospective therapists, I found one who seemed to understand and who was able to help me begin to deal with my grief over the betrayal by my parents, the trauma of psychiatric abuse, and the loss of my trust in the world. Art was a respected therapist in the Austin community, and during the three years I worked with him, I experienced major healing. With Art's encouragement, I requested the records from the hospital in Birmingham, but after several inquiries, I found I could only do so by going through an attorney.

My search for external facts and evidence about my experiences was fueled by the need to understand how it all had fit together, to know why and how this could have happened. Having forgotten many details, and not wanting to imagine anything that had not actually happened, I felt it was important to continue my quest: to find the truth of what had happened to me and, as much as I could, free myself from it.

I flew to Birmingham over spring break and stayed with my friend Irini and her husband while pursuing answers to my many questions. Peggy, my roommate from Birmingham Southern and Peggy's husband, Michael, helped me revisit places in Birmingham that were scenes of the original trauma. We drove around the college campus, and to the hospital where I had been incarcerated those five weeks as a teenager.

The old mansion, once the outpatient and office building, had been demolished, but the admissions building looked familiar. I even worked up the courage to walk in alone and ask to see a patient, claiming I was a friend of someone whose name I had invented.

I also made an appointment to see Dr. William Hawley, my mother's doctor, who had originally recommended Larkin for my dad. He listened carefully as I told him of my parents' years of drinking, their kidnapping me from the airport, and the horror of five weeks in the hospital, followed by three more years of shocks. Dr. Hawley told me that he had had no idea that I had ever been admitted to the hospital, much less that I had been shocked another three years after my release. My mother had told him only about the first summer of shocks, in 1965 before I left for the University of Michigan.

His advice was to enjoy my life with Tom and my achievements and live my life. He did understand why I was trying to find out as much as I could, and said it was a healthy impulse, but when I inquired about Larkin's dismissal, he seemed reluctant to say anything, remarking that he had "not had much to do with the folks at that hospital" for many years. Soon after I returned to Austin, I received a letter from Dr. Hawley, written the same day I had met with him. The letter consisted of a single paragraph:

Dear Julia:

I appreciate your coming to see me to clarify many things about you and your family. I trust the interview helped to relieve, at least temporarily, some of your tensions. Please believe me when I say I am certain your interpretation with respect to the content to be true. Please call on me as you will.

Sincerely,
William L. Hawley, M.D.

Just as the strange tour of Birmingham with Peggy and Michael helped me confront old fears, Dr. Hawley's letter was a welcome validation of how I saw the past. Yet it was not enough to lighten the grief that always shadowed me as I tried to piece events together so that they made sense, not only as a sequenced narrative, but also as the rationale behind my mother's allowing Larkin to shock me for so many years.

Tom and I drove out to California that summer and visited Paul and his wife Polly, the first time I had seen Paul in over thirteen years. They were helpful and supportive, and Paul told me that when he had first started practicing in Texas he was astounded at the number of people, usually women, who had been summarily labeled insane or schizophrenic, then forced or coerced into electroshock and drugs.

Back in Austin, we moved into the university's married student apartments and I continued my quest for the truth in therapy with Art. I began the new fall semester of my graduate studies – writing papers, giving presentations, and working as a teaching assistant. Finishing the PhD was important to me. The graduate program gave me goals for future success, while my personal quest sought the truth about what had happened to me.

One exercise that often helps people heal from abuse is writing a letter to the perpetrator. Usually the letter is never sent and healing comes primarily from articulating the words needed to confront the abuser. I didn't think that merely writing a letter to Larkin would help me as much as writing and actually sending one. So I sent the letter certified, restricted signature required, and in the return address I used Tom's name (Mrs. Thomas Welton).

I tried to say what I thought Larkin should hear. I couldn't bring myself to use the salutation "Dear," so I began the letter with a bald use of his name:

Harold Larkin:

I am writing to you to say many things. As a minor, I was a patient of yours against my will almost twenty years ago, and I

*want to confront you with my knowledge of the fact of your
mistreatment of me.*

I told him that I was glad he had been fired from the hospital and
that I hoped he had been censured by the state board of medical
examiners. I continued the letter:

What you did to me and to others was morally wrong.
What you subjected me and others to was an atrocity.
You should be forced to confront and acknowledge what you did.

Following accusations that he had treated me and others irrespon-
sibly and that he had not regarded us as fellow human beings, I
tried to shame him. I made it clear that I had found other physicians who disagreed with him and helped me to discontinue all
psychotropic drugs by 1975. I ended the letter with the strongest
reproach I could imagine:

*I hope this letter has made clear to you that at least one of your
former patients saw your actions clearly during the period of your
abuse of her and remained strong enough to confront you by
calling what you did by its true name.*
Very sincerely yours,
Emilie Julia Hoeffler Welton

The green card with Larkin's signature came by return mail. I
had not expected him to answer, but the signed card showed he
had at least received the letter, if not read it.

I had hoped that sending the letter and confronting Larkin
directly would bring noticeable relief, but it did not. Late at night
I would sometimes be in such emotional pain I would go downstairs to the parking lot, lock myself in the car, and rant into a
tape recorder. I never listened to the tapes, but having a tape
recorder on made me feel that perhaps someday someone would
listen to what I was saying. Gradually, this grieving into the tape
recorder transformed into a type of prayer new to me: a lament, a
spontaneous outpouring of the heart.

In October 1987 the American Musicological Society was meeting in New Orleans. Dealing with the past trauma was taking its toll, and I was considering taking a leave from graduate school or even dropping out of the program. But something strange happened that I took as a sign to continue.

The AMS was holding a raffle to raise money for scholarships, offering a complete set of the premier encyclopedia of music, the 1981 *New Grove Dictionary of Music and Musicians,* to the winner. I decided to buy five chances. As I was writing the check in my university office, I suddenly felt an uncanny fear when I knew, unmistakably, that I was going to win the prize. It was as if somehow I had seen into something we are not normally allowed to see. Although the fear faded somewhat as I continued through the day, it did not disappear.

At the registration desk for the New Orleans convention I purchased two more raffle tickets. By now I only half believed I would win, but I kept the newly purchased tickets in a separate part of my purse. In case I won, I could tell which set of tickets had held the winning one.

On the last night of the meeting, I attended the dance where the drawing for the door prize was to be held. Sure enough, I held the winning ticket, and I felt goose bumps when I realized the ticket came from the first set. I took it as a sign not to take a leave of absence or quit graduate school.

One of the most healing things in those years was joining the church choir directed by Douglass Green, one of my graduate professors. Tom was offered a job in Austin soon after, and he also joined. The choir's camaraderie centered around Doug. Tom and I enjoyed the choir's many Sunday dinners at Doug and Marquita's home, dinners where the hosts and guests had real conversations, where no one was drunk or bullying anyone else. The first night I attended rehearsal, Mendelssohn's "Blessed are they that have endured," from his oratorio *Saint Paul,* was the first piece we rehearsed. I took this as a sign and worked to hold back my tears as we sang.

On another visit to Birmingham I saw an attorney who was able to obtain my medical records from the hospital files. Although Larkin was no longer at the hospital, my records were still on file. They had been microfilmed in June 1973, the date Irini's friend had reported Larkin's dismissal. The records were sent to Art, but he gave the package to me, acknowledging my right to know what had been done to me and written about me.

I drove home from Art's office and decided to start reading that evening. Holding the thick manila mailer in my hands, I felt a mixture of eager curiosity and foreboding. Inside the package was a stack of grey, standard sized printouts from the microfilm. Reading through these pages – some reproductions of typewriter print, some of handwritten notes – would turn into a laborious, time-consuming process. There were copies of telephone messages, letters Larkin had written to other doctors, reports of interviews with my mother and dad, and nurse's notes.

Buried somewhere was the document I most wanted to see: the log of electroshocks. Skimming through quickly, I found it. Now I could finally know exactly how many there had been: sixty-six. Art had suggested that knowing the concrete details – the drugs prescribed, the number of treatments, the things Larkin had written about me – would help me gain a sense of control over what had happened.

Over the next several days, I continued reading, finding much that shed light on what had happened to me. Arranging these impersonal notes, letters, and logs into a precise chronology brought my memories into sharper focus.

Larkin's note from June 1965 labeled me with his initial impression: schizophrenia, based on the inconclusive report from the psychologist who had administered the paper and pencil tests.[46] In 1972 when I moved to Houston and was no longer officially his patient, however, he closed the file by listing my diagnosis as adolescent adjustment reaction, often termed the "common cold" of teenagers who enter counseling.[47]

Through the alumni association, I contacted a woman I had known briefly at Birmingham Southern who had also been a patient of Larkin's. Barbara had endured not only many electroshocks but even more damaging insulin shock treatments. She told me her own records showed the same two diagnoses – at the beginning and over a year later at the end. Larkin's changing a severe diagnosis to something so innocuous, Art pointed out, signaled something suspicious.

Reading, transcribing, and emotionally processing the records was a stressful experience, but Art's support helped me persevere. I diligently transcribed every line of the records, making many trips to the library to look up each drug that had been given to me, every term I did not understand. Art was correct: although it was distressing to read these things that had been done to me, the young woman I had been so long ago, I felt a growing sense of freedom as I learned more of the truth of what had happened.

The records were not complete, I realized, when I found that the form I so clearly remembered signing upon admission was absent; nevertheless, many items were quite revealing, including reports from a social worker at the hospital. From an interview with my mother two days after my admission, she reported, "Mrs. Hoeffler appeared to be extremely cooperative, and I got the impression that she will be willing to go along with the medical staff suggestions and there will be no trouble as far as treatment to the patient is concerned." Reading this, I could easily imagine my mother giving the hospital carte blanche to shock me, as she sometimes put it, "to root out" my supposed problems.

Other notes showed Mother's concern about my success in college. The social worker wrote, "Mrs. Hoeffler would like to mention that she thinks Julia is probably too heavily sedated as Julia is complaining that she can't think, she is having difficulty in concentrating at school, and at times she is asleep by 8:00 every evening." And one note on the day of my forty-first electroshock, recorded, "Doing better [come back in] 1 week. Mother says leave Thorazine off before exam."

As I read through the records, Larkin's words often sounded like my mother's. I realized that she must have talked to him more than I knew, and there was detailed information that could only have come from her. A grim irony emerged: he never treated me or even who he thought I was, but my mother's projection of me.

One night that spring in Austin I dreamed about the burglar who tried to break into our house when I was four. Someone was trying to get in the window. I heard a noise and looked out the window. Suddenly afraid, I saw a man's hand on the window sill. He was prying open the window with some kind of knife. He smiled at me, threateningly, and talked to me through the window in a sing song voice. His light auburn hair, freckles, and face were so vivid that even today I could easily complete a composite picture of him for the police. He held out a deck of cards to me saying, "Deal?" Then he bent the deck and the cards flew out one after another, as in cartoons I had seen as a child.

That same night I had another nightmare in which I was a few years older. A woman grabbed me from behind and held me around my neck while cutting off my hair in back, my childhood braids. It felt like she was using a razor blade, scraping off my hair and that she might injure my brain, cutting through my scalp with the blade. Because she held me so tightly, all I could see was the woman's shoes. But the shoes and feet looked like Mother's, and the voice was unmistakably hers. As she sheared off my braids, she kept repeating, "You think you're so smart! You think you're so smart!"

Mother never liked having to re-braid my hair in the morning before school. It felt as if she resented any little thing she had to do to take care of me, but more likely she was so deeply unhappy that she had nothing to give. I had loved my braids and had been proud of them. I felt pretty with my braids.

The morning after the nightmares, I had to be on campus early to practice before my piano lesson with my teacher, Claire. Climbing the stairs to the practice room, I was exhausted from lack of sleep and from the emotional impact of the dreams. Twice I tripped and caught myself on the stairs with my arms. In the practice room, I sat down at the piano, and all of a sudden my body seemed to split in two separate people. I saw one stand up next to the piano bench. I remained sitting at the keyboard. She started hitting me back and forth across my face, saying "You think you're so smart! I'll show you!" repeatedly, while hitting me again and again.

I somehow managed to walk down the stairs to my piano lesson a few minutes later. As Claire began encouraging me to play from the shoulders to loosen up in order to get a better tone, I burst into tears and put my hands over my face: I could not continue after what had happened in the practice room. Claire, the epitome of a good teacher, talked softly to me and did not try to get me to play. Claire knew intuitively the best way to help me. I became calmer and was able to leave the building.

As I drove home from the lesson, still shaken, I kept asking myself, had it been a hallucination? Was I really mentally ill after all?

When I spoke to Art about what had happened, he told me it had not been a hallucination, but a flashback, and I realized it must be a memory of my mother. Although I hadn't previously remembered Mother ever losing control, I had always remembered the bare fact that she had cut off my braids. When I had talked to her about it as an adult, Mother had claimed I had somehow cut them halfway off so that when she went to rebraid them one morning, they fell off in her hands. She cut them off the rest of the way and took me for a permanent.

That part might have been true, but Mother left out how she lost her temper and struck me repeatedly because she was angry about my causing her extra trouble. And as she cut them the rest of the way off before she took me for the permanent, I would have experienced the shearing off of my braids as I felt in the dream.

The contradiction between what my mother had told me and what I had experienced in the dream and flashback made me determined to reconstruct what had happened as accurately as possible. I contacted my friends Beverly and Cathie, who both remembered coming by my family's house that day to see if I could come out to play. They remembered my mother telling them that I was in my room and did not want to come out, but they could go in and ask me.

Beverly remembered seeing me, despondent yet very angry at my mother, curled up in the little space between the bed and the dresser. The atmosphere in the house, she recalled, was threatening, with my mother "lurking in the background like a velociraptor." The look in my eyes, she said, had haunted her ever since. She and her sister Cathie had not understood why I was so distressed and angry at my mother. Cathie told me they had thought getting a professional haircut and perm would be a great thing.

I found further confirmation in some letters I had saved from fifth grade. These were letters from Miss Rogers, who had taught Cathie and me in fourth grade but had moved to New York the following year. In a letter from March 1958, Miss Rogers wrote: "You know I always enjoy hearing from you. Your last letter didn't look like the letters you usually write me. What happened? Let's remember what pretty writing you did for me last year."

Apparently I had not told Miss Rogers anything about the incident, but my emotional reaction was clear from my handwriting. The next month after a visit home to Birmingham, Miss Rogers wrote, "Enjoyed seeing my girl at Easter. I like your hair cut short, so keep it that way at least for a while."

I spoke again with my aunt who had told me about my mother's "nervous breakdown" when I was ten years old, and discovered that this had occurred in the spring, which correlated with Miss Rogers' letter mentioning Easter and with Grandma Miller's visit. I concluded that Mother must have been frightened by the strength of her reaction and had called Grandma to come to Birmingham to help her keep things under control.

This evidence from Beverly, Cathie, Miss Rogers' letters, and my aunt freed me from the fear that I had merely imagined the entire incident. The flashback in the practice room had been a memory of something that really happened, not a hallucination.

In light of the rage towards my mother, I was grateful to be seeing a therapist who could help me deal with frightening emotions, but I knew that one type of therapy in vogue at the time would not work for me. One theory propounded by advocates of codependency therapy demanded that people with psychological injuries "had" to forgive their abusers, if only for the victims' own good. Unfortunately, Art himself held this view.

To be told I "had" to forgive my mother was unacceptable. I sought support by reading an ever increasing number of books, but most held that a victim would be better off if she "forgave" her abusers. While some took different approaches to forgiveness, none brought a satisfying answer. Trapped in an endless cycle of rage at my Mother and Larkin for what they had done, yet feeling deeply guilty, even condemned, for harboring such anger, I could not reconcile the two.

But one book I read, *The Hiding Place* by Corrie ten Boom, was different.[48] During World War II, her family hid a number of Jews in their home near Amsterdam. Someone reported her family to the Gestapo and they were put in prison and interrogated. Their elderly father died in prison, but the two sisters were sent together to a concentration camp. There, they lived out their faith, comforting other prisoners and each other in beautiful ways. Corrie's sister died in the camp, but through a clerical error, Corrie was released.

After the war, Corrie set about trying to help people heal from their experiences. She set up homes where traumatized war victims could heal. She also traveled across Europe preaching forgiveness and healing.

One Sunday she had preached in a church, and as usual, people were filing out, shaking her hand and thanking her for her words of healing. Suddenly she saw a man she immediately recognized as one of the camp guards coming toward her to take her hand. "How marvelous that Christ has forgiven even me," he said. Corrie stood there paralyzed. She could not will herself to raise her hand to shake his. She prayed silently "Lord Jesus, help me to forgive this man." She could not raise her hand, and she prayed a second time: "Lord Jesus, please help me to forgive this man." Still her hand remained frozen at her side. She desperately prayed a third time, "Lord Jesus, I cannot forgive him, give me your forgiveness."

Then, without her will being involved, her arm rose from her side and she was able to shake the man's hand, and she felt a marvelous sense of healing and forgiveness coming from outside herself. That was when she realized that forgiveness is a gift of grace.

One evening I attended a church healing retreat where the priest said that often the reason people are not healed is that they have a block in their souls because they have not forgiven someone for a wrong. The priest's words cut deep; as I left the retreat and drove home, I was angry not only at my mother, but also at people who serenely preach forgiveness but who have never had to forgive such a betrayal.

I called Pastor Peterman long distance. He remarked that normally he was not at home on that particular weeknight, so God must be at work. I told him about the scene in Corrie ten Boom's book, and about what the priest at the retreat had said. "But Julia," he said, "your mother is not walking up to you holding out her hand!" He continued, telling me that forgiveness has many definitions and that in his view it takes two to forgive: I could not forgive my mother unless she asked for forgiveness.

I prayed about it every night, feeling like I must be an evil person because of all the rage and hatred. Yet I still yearned for a soft word from my mother, for her to care about what she had done to me.

Pastor Peterman gave me the name of Pastor Johnson in Austin. A wonderful man, he met with me once or twice a week for almost two years. He always saw me either the day I called or the following day. He helped me with many questions of faith.

I had trouble with the Lord's Prayer – I could not say the one petition, "Forgive us our sins as we forgive those who sin against us." Pastor Johnson told me to bracket that phrase regarding my mother for the time being. He said forgiveness was a process, and that I should not feel guilty for where I was in that process.

Sometimes I fantasized about getting a phone call telling me my father and mother had both been killed in an accident. That I would feel relief at such news filled me with horror and guilt. Yet the rage and pain were so overwhelming that I had to stop all contact with them.

"Now you aren't sticking any pins into voodoo dolls or anything," Pastor Johnson said, "and you aren't planning to kill them, are you?" And of course I wasn't. "Well, as long as it doesn't progress to that, I don't think you have anything to worry about," he replied.

Even so, I was hesitant to take communion. An Episcopal priest I had asked about it told me that it was OK to go to the altar even troubled by fear and guilt, that God loves us no matter how we feel. He said there was a certain kind of healing in the sacrament itself, enacted at a table where all are welcome guests.

One Sunday, sitting as usual near the altar in the choir, I let my mind wander on its own paths during the long prayer the priest says before the communion. By some grace, I reached a point I later called "authentic surrender." I was enabled to pray, sincerely and devoutly, Corrie ten Boom's prayer: "Lord, I cannot forgive my mother, please give me your forgiveness."

I felt dizzy. I was not sure I could make it to the communion rail, but I walked slowly and managed to kneel. While I was waiting, my eyes half closed, for the priest distributing the bread, I sensed Mother's presence as if she were kneeling next to me, waiting to receive the sacrament.

7. ... AND BEING PUT BACK TOGETHER

Lord I am not worthy to receive you, but only say the word and I shall be healed.[49]

– Preparatory Communion Prayer

After the turning point of my experience at the communion rail, my quest for truth took a new direction, leading to more healing through new relationships and frameworks for understanding what had happened to me. I changed to a new therapist, Marie. An excellent psychologist, she was the model of a compassionate, caring woman. Paul had suggested that perhaps it was time for me to work with a woman, and Art agreed that such a change might benefit me in dealing more clearly with my feelings about my mother.

My friendship with Jocelynn, a woman twenty-one years older whom I had known since graduate school in English, was another source of healing in my life. She and I had begun what Tom dubbed a series of "film binges and gabfests" a few years earlier when she was recovering from surgery. Her husband and son were due to take their annual fishing trip but didn't want to leave her alone. I offered to stay with her in Houston, and Jocelynn and I made the occasion into something special.

An enthusiastic film buff, Jocelynn had grown up in Los Angeles in the 1930s and 40s and had known many people in the film industry. Our discussions ran late into the night as we explored questions raised by the films we watched together in her home theater room. And every time I visited Jocelynn for one of our film binges, I also made an appointment with Pastor Peterman to continue our talks about healing and forgiveness.

Through discussion with Marie, I realized that the process I had been going through all this time was one of grieving. Although I was not grieving for a specific, easily recognizable loss as in the death of a family member, I was grieving for the loss of many things.

A friend in one of my graduate classes loaned me a book, *Life is Goodbye, Life is Hello: Grieving Well Through All Kinds of Loss,* and this also helped me understand that healing from trauma was, for me, a type of grieving.[50] Marie helped me identify the losses of more than a decade of my life to psychiatric abuse and its aftereffects of nightmares and flashbacks. I had also lost many memories, the ability to sleep restfully, and my healthy body, but I had lost what many people take for granted: my basic assumption about the world as a good and beautiful place as well as any trust in my parents and in most medical doctors.[51]

After Marie told me about a monastery in Pecos, New Mexico, with a retreat ministry of healing, I traveled there several times to continue my quest. I was assigned a spiritual director, Sr. Gabriella. In our daily talks I began to see my traumatic experiences in the broader context of a spiritual life.

Many at the retreats needed healing from illness, immense grief, or trauma, and telling each other our stories was a healing experience in itself. In its serene mountain setting, the monastery was an ideal place for people helping each other heal and grow, physically, emotionally, and spiritually.

During breaks from the talks and small group sessions, groups of two or three would take leisurely walks around the lake or through the woods. In the winter after a fresh snowfall, the new snow crunching underfoot, I relished the unhurried pace talking with a companion or two and breathing the crisp, clean air.

One retreat centered on a healing exercise through physical movement. As meditative Taizé music played, Sr. Gabriella explained, we were to walk in a large circle. Anyone could go into the center and express thanksgiving, joy, or a need for healing, but only through the language of movement or dance. We could also enact a need of someone we knew or any prayer concern.

Those of us still in the circle prayed silently for the people in the center, or we could respond to one of them, eventually leading them back into the circle to join the community of prayerful walkers. Some depicted hunger, while others expressed grief, despair, or fear. One woman curled up tightly on the floor with her eyes closed. A priest from Oregon moved into the center of the circle and began a beautiful, slow freeform dance of praise, raising his arms and turning in circles.

A dark-haired woman in the center was gesturing as if she were wiping away tears. She then covered her face with her hands and began rocking back and forth. I went into the center and placed my hand gently on her arm. She held my hand as I made a gesture of wiping her tears away, offering her an embrace. As I guided her back into the community of walkers, my own tears increased to barely stifled sobs.

I didn't feel brave enough to move into the center of the circle myself, but I saw the woman as enacting my own pain and grief, and through ministering to her, I was also helping myself express my pain and heal from it.

Another retreat focused on centering prayer, a contemplative practice whose objective is to open the mind and heart quietly to God rather than speak to God in need, sorrow, or thanksgiving. The idea is to "wait for God," becoming aware of God's presence and being receptive to God's will.[52] As I began to practice this type of prayer back home, it gradually bore fruit, and I felt somewhat at peace.

Singing in Doug's church choir provided good music, friends, and community, and I also made progress toward the doctorate by sitting for three language exams, completing my coursework, and preparing for comprehensive exams.

I also became friends with Evelyn, one of our neighbors in married student housing. Evelyn had been raped and stabbed by an intruder in her own home a few years before and was having difficulty functioning at work. Her psychiatrist had advised her to have shock treatments and through mutual friends she came to me. Evelyn and I had many conversations, always discussing the ways to heal from our respective traumas, even as she was subjected to shock treatments that left severe memory loss. She told me that the next day after one of her treatments she had gone to the grocery store but couldn't remember how to get home and drove around for two hours trying to find the way.

In March 1993, my father was alone in the house in Birmingham when the "winter hurricane" hit. Mother was playing bridge at a downtown hotel and Dad told her not to risk the drive home in the storm. Wind and ice had toppled many trees, collapsing power lines and cutting off electricity to many homes in the area.

Dad went next door to check on an elderly neighbor but fell on the way home, apparently pulling himself through the snow and crawling to the back door. He called 911 and when the EMS men arrived, he had recovered enough from falling to tell them he preferred to ride out the storm at home. Shortly after, the electricity went out and the phone lines went down.

My brother tried to call Dad several times from Tennessee, but never got through and assumed this was because the phones were out from the storm. Mother could not make it home until late the next morning, only to find him lying on the bedroom floor in the freezing cold. His shoulder was shattered after falling while trying to plug in a telephone next to the bed.

I was able to fly to Birmingham and see him in the ICU, as did his two sisters and my brother. One evening when the rest of the family had left, I was grateful to be alone with him. "It wasn't your fault," I told him quietly. But since he could not speak, there was no way I could tell if he understood me. I was also grateful to be there to request pain medication when he was visibly hurting and to assure him it was on the way.

Mother left to sign some forms and when Dad died, the only people present were one of my cousins and me. We were in one of several small rooms just off the ICU where patients who were about to die were moved. I held Dad's hand, made the sign of the cross on his forehead, and prayed out loud, "Lord, receive the soul of your son, Bill. Take him home to you and heal and comfort him from everything that has harmed him. Heal him and make him whole."

His memorial service was difficult. Although the minister of our old church spoke at the service, Mother had it held in the funeral home. She was adamant about having no hymns. Three years later, when Grandma was dying, Mother wrote me that she hated hearing organ music because it made her want to cry, reminding her of the coming loss of her own mother. Once again I saw how afraid she was of feeling strong emotion herself and sought to control or avoid it, and how she appeared to have little empathy for the strong emotions of others.

It meant a lot that Peggy, Irini, and Despina came to the funeral and that Beverly and Cathie sent flowers to the house. Tom made it to Birmingham in time for the service and brought a mass of silk bluebonnets for a prominently placed floral arrangement. One of my dad's friends, Saul Cooley, a member of the Magic City Gun Club with my dad, recognized me and spoke kindly to me. I managed to be polite to my mother and brother, and it helped that Elizabeth, Dad's youngest sister, had come from Oklahoma. During several long conversations while Dad was in the hospital, Aunt Elizabeth told me she knew about Dad's and Mother's excessive drinking.

The minister read Dad's obituary and preached a eulogy. Part of the "greatest generation," my father was driven by duty, beginning his freshman year in college straight from the farm at sixteen, marrying at twenty, and completing a doctoral degree at twenty-seven on the heels of a world war. He had taught a generation of students and had seen many changes in the medical school.

As the service continued, I began to think how Dad was a victim of a primitive psychiatric system, incorrectly diagnosed with a mental illness and prescribed debilitating drugs for more than thirty years, his alcoholism never recognized, except fleetingly by himself.

Once on a visit to Birmingham in the early 1980s I was talking to Irini on the phone in my parents' kitchen. After their usual drinks, Mother and Dad had both gone to sleep, but my dad woke up and came into the kitchen in his pajamas and robe, wanting to talk. I greeted him, Irini still on the line. "You know," he said, "I think your mother and I are both alcoholics." I will always regret that I did not cut short my phone call and advise him to seek help. Perhaps if I had listened to him and urged him to join AA something would have come of it.

Although my dad was not the best father, I am grateful that I can remember what his voice sounded like and the times he spoke to me with warmth, pride, and love. This surprises me, in light of the many memories I have of his anger, his drinking, and his often cruel teasing, but he did, somehow, communicate his love. I wish he could have had a better chance at life, one with opportunities for healing such as I experienced at the Pecos monastery, but that was not to be.

After the funeral, some of the cousins came to Birmingham for a few days to visit. Mother seemed in control, but underneath, I could tell she was in turmoil over the sudden loss. Tom and I stayed with Irini and her husband to allow room in the house for my cousins. After a few days, we returned to Texas.

The next month, a book catalogue arrived in the mail with an advertisement for *The Scapegoat* by the French literature scholar René Girard.[53] Sensing that had been my role in our family, I was always on the lookout for books using the term. None of the ones I had read were very helpful, and I did not expect this new book to help either, but I ordered it anyway.

The book was so compelling that I stayed up all night to finish it. According to Girard, a threatened or conflicted group will unconsciously try to unify its members by singling out a scapegoat, a member of the group deemed responsible for the group's problems. Persons most likely to be scapegoated are those who are vulnerable or different in some way.

As the youngest in my family, with alcoholic parents perpetually on the verge of divorce and an older brother no longer at home, I was a natural scapegoat. My unhappiness at breaking up with my first boyfriend and my lack of power in the family structure, plus the normal vulnerabilities of an emotional teenager, had worked together to act as an unconscious lightning rod for my parents' animosity toward each other. They could unite in focusing on their supposedly "mentally ill" daughter, and thus ignore or deny their own deeper conflicts.

In primitive sacrifices of scapegoats, even the scapegoat had to appear to agree that he or she needed to be sacrificed.[54] This resonated for me with the necessity to deaden myself and acquiesce to the shocks, to appear as if I accepted Larkin's and my family's view that I needed this violent treatment to restore me to my family.

I also came to understand that acquiescing to the original abuse was somehow intertwined with giving in to the demand to forgive my abusers. Although to survive, I had to maintain the appearance of accepting Larkin's diagnosis and treatments, I had never done so willingly. Thus a demand to forgive my abusers was tantamount to the equally unacceptable demand to view Larkin's abuse as legitimate medical treatment that had not harmed me.

I obtained the rest of Girard's books and read them one by one. Each book built on the last toward a deeper understanding of scapegoating. After reading Girard's *Job: A Victim of His People*, I wrote directly to Girard in care of his publishers, thanking him for his books and telling him my own story of scapegoating.

René replied by return post with an encouraging letter, and Tom and I joined COV&R, the Colloquium on Violence and Religion,[55] founded to study and develop Girard's theory.

Tom and I regularly attended meetings of the Colloquium; I was elected to the board and served as treasurer for ten years. I enjoyed working for the organization, becoming friends with its members, all drawn to the redemptive vision of Girard's theory.

Through all this reading and discussion with friends, therapists, and clergy, I learned what to me was most important about forgiveness. Forgiveness may often be defined as an act of the will, but in emotional terms, I see it as a surrender, a passive giving over of the will to God rather than an overt act: I cannot surrender my will through an act of the will. Forgiveness is a process, and when it happens, it is a gift of healing from God.

During these years of being put back together I found much healing as a member of several communities focused on helping and healing others: the choir, the colloquium, the community of graduate students working toward common goals, the monastery and the church. It seemed that everywhere I had friends who understood and valued me both for myself and for my work.

One friendship, however, had a tragic ending. Evelyn, whom I had tried so hard to help heal from her traumatic experiences, succeeded after several attempts in killing herself.

8. RESTORATIVE JUSTICE OR STALEMATE?

Victims also desperately need what might be called an 'experience of justice.' It is often assumed that vengeance is primary to this need, but many studies suggest that the desire for vengeance often springs from a feeling that justice has been denied... Victims need opportunities to tell their stories and to vent their feelings, often repeatedly, to people who matter, to friends, to those in law-enforcement, perhaps even to those who caused this pain. And they need answers to the questions that haunt them: Why me? What could I have done differently? What kind of person did this and why? Without answers, it can be very difficult to restore a sense of order and therefore to heal. The restorative paradigm of justice sees crime as a violation of people and relationships. Wrongs create obligations to make things right. Shalom – right relationships – are the goal.[56]

—Howard Zehr

For two years I tried to persuade my mother to go for counseling. At first I tried simple requests: "Would you consider going to talk to a counselor?" Mother's response was always negative, so I stepped up my requests to something closer to a demand: "I want you to go see a counselor." Or "Please go see a counselor." But Mother only became more adamant in her refusals.

Finally, I concluded that to survive emotionally I would have to break completely from my mother unless she sought counseling. I suggested that she find someone in the Dallas area – she had moved to Dallas the year after my dad died – and begin to see a counselor on her own. This way, I reasoned, she could develop a healing rapport with a therapist and later feel more comfortable in a joint session.

I gave my mother an ultimatum – if she didn't see a counselor at least six times before including me in a session, I would never have any contact with her again. "OK," she replied, "I'll find other things to do with my time."

For five months there was no contact between us, and my heart ached from the rejection I felt. When my friend Evelyn succeeded in killing herself, I felt bereft and guilty. I had tried to help her for so long and now berated myself for not saying the right thing the night Evelyn had called me telling me she was going to do it. After the funeral, Evelyn's husband, Peter, assured me that Evelyn had made calls that evening to many different people and that nothing I could have said or done could have prevented the suicide.

Peter's assurance couldn't stop me from feeling I should have done more or said something different. One night I broke my resolve and called my mother, telling her that Evelyn had killed herself because she did not want to be subjected to any more shock treatments. Mother's response was a total surprise. She said that she had begun seeing a counselor, Christa, a minister at her church trained in pastoral counseling.

Tom and I had to leave for Italy for me to work with the manuscript I was researching for my dissertation. Upon our return, I contacted my mother's counselor and arranged for the three of us to meet. I prayed about the matter and tried very hard to approach the encounter without rancor or any desire for revenge. During the meeting I tried not to say anything intended to hurt my mother's feelings, but it was difficult. This initial session lasted over three hours, at Christa's home office, with Tom waiting in the living room reading and working with his computer listings.

I was aware that Mother had suffered a mild stroke earlier that year, so I tried to suppress my anger. But her denial and manner of speaking made it extremely difficult to edit my words and avoid lashing back at her with a desire to hurt. Christa was a good facilitator and guided the session gently. But Mother denied everything. She "did not say," then "did not remember saying" the hurtful words I remembered. She strongly denied the extent of their drinking, and said that she and Dad had never had more than one or two drinks a night.

The session was not a brilliant success. Although I was able to recognize Mother's significant gesture in seeing Christa, the pain did not diminish, especially in the face of my mother's denials.

I realized that all those years after the shocks when Mother would visit in Houston or when I went to Birmingham I had created a false persona. Laboring under the need to maintain some kind of relationship with my family, I had suppressed my own need to confront her about what had happened, to ask her how she could have done it, how she could have let Larkin begin the shocks and continue them for more than three years, and then why he had stopped. All that time I knew she had lied to Irini that night in Houston and had manipulated the situation for her own ends, but I was too afraid to confront her. If I wanted to maintain a relationship with my original family, I had to pretend to be a good adult daughter, to act as if nothing bad had ever happened.

In a letter before the next meeting, Christa asked me what I needed or wanted from my mother. Groping to articulate my answer, I replied, "Specifically I need for her to acknowledge that what she did was wrong and that she hurt me. It doesn't matter if she knew it was wrong at the time, but she has never admitted that she understands now that any of it was wrong."

Christa also had asked me what I would have said if I could have reached my mother on the phone the night back in 1968 when I would have killed myself but for Jim's phone call. "I am not sure I would have been able to even say it back in 1968," I answered, "because they would probably have had me shocked extra if I had called and cried, which I most certainly would have done if I could have talked to them that night. I would have seemed 'upset' to them and 'disturbed' and 'crazy' if I had gotten them on the phone that night, because what I needed to tell them was 'Please make Larkin stop hurting me. He is hurting me and it is killing me. I am not crazy. Please stop drinking and get some counseling for yourselves and for me. Please make him stop hurting me.' And maybe it is good that I was not able to reach them that night, because if I had they would probably have had me hurt more for being 'upset.'" Christa wrote in reply that she appreciated my letter and that it helped her to understand and prepare my mother for another meeting.

I drove up to Dallas by myself for the second meeting with Christa and Mother. After I stopped in Waxahachie for lunch, I realized I was well ahead of my schedule and decided to find a church where I could pray about the upcoming session. The door to the Episcopal church was locked, but the Catholic church down the street was open, and something was going on inside. It was not a formal liturgy, just people praying, so I joined them and prayed for God to help me maintain a positive approach to the meeting, for God to help me avoid wanting revenge.

I lit a candle and left the church for the parking lot. There was a soccer field for the parish school nearby, and a match was about to begin. A group of women were chatting in the parking lot. "Typical soccer moms," I thought.

I had been upset while praying and must have still looked emotional. I had to pass the soccer moms to get to my car, and one of the women asked me if I were all right. I replied yes, and then, my voice breaking, said that I was going to Dallas for a meeting with my mother. The women probably imagined I was an adopted child going to meet my birth mother for the first time, but I didn't want to go into any detail.

One of the women asked me if I would like them to pray for me and I said yes. The woman fixed her eye on me and said, "You're not Catholic, are you?" I replied, "No, I'm not." The woman said, "Well, prayer is prayer, so that doesn't matter, does it?" I agreed, and the soccer moms gathered around me, placing their hands on my head, shoulders, and arms. They began praying, gently singing in tongues, something I was familiar with from my retreats at Pecos monastery. I thanked the women and left, feeling a lifting of my spirits, and hoping that this meeting with Christa and Mother would go better than the last one had.

The second session was slightly more successful than the first. When I related my memory of how she and Dad kidnapped me from the airport and took me to the mental hospital, my mother, surprised, said, "We thought you had forgotten that. You never talked about it." I replied, "Well, Larkin probably told you I wouldn't remember it – it is quite unusual for anyone to remember how they got to the hospital, but that is just one more thing he was wrong about. And as to why I never talked about it, I was afraid to say anything, because it was upsetting to me to think about it and if I had talked about it I might have cried and you might have decided I needed more shock treatments."

"Why must you insist on continuing your misery-seeking resurrection of the past?" Mother asked, "And why can't you focus on the good things?" "I'm sorry," I replied as gently as I could, "but I have very few good memories."

She couldn't understand that my "resurrection of the past" was the only way to know the truth and be freed from its pain. Her need to defend herself, to maintain that *it wasn't her fault*, overrode all else. Nevertheless, she had tried: she had counseled privately with Christa and had been willing to meet with me.

Ultimately, the two meetings did accomplish something positive. I could now be around my mother for limited periods of time, provided Tom was always present as a buffer. Tom was willing to act in this capacity, and did so for the next twelve years.

When Grandma died at age 100, I was able to attend the funeral and be polite, although I didn't feel comfortable around my mother, cousins, uncles, and aunts. I never knew what Mother might have said to her brothers or their wives, or what my cousins knew about my teenage years. Once a stigmatizing label such as "mentally ill" has been officially applied, a person is continuously on guard about who knows the secret and who does not, and how he or she will be judged when interacting with others.[57]

Mother did try to make it up, perhaps – with money. She helped us buy a house and car, and gave us money for exceptional expenses. (She did similar things for my brother and his wife, always trying to be fair and equal.) Although the gifts were welcome, I still yearned for an explicit acknowledgement of the damage done to me and for my mother to take responsibility for what she had done, to understand how deeply I had been hurt by the shocks and drugs.

After completing the PhD, I worked several years at part-time teaching jobs for Elderhostel and other continuing education programs through the University of Texas. Eventually I was hired on a two-year contract as an assistant professor at the University of Louisville, a post which required living in Louisville for ten months of each year and making several round trips to Austin. Tom and I would stop by Dallas in each direction and eat lunch with Mother, my brother, and sister-in-law, and we made a yearly Christmas visit. Hearing her voice evoked painful emotions and memories, and Tom noticed that I seemed troubled and sad for one or two days after each contact with my mother.

At least I could see some effort toward reconciliation in her willingness to see Christa as well as her gifts of money, and I could still feel compassion for my mother's failing health and advancing age.

Mother came up to Louisville just before my second semester began. One afternoon she was trying to help me staple copies of the syllabus for one of my classes. Mother's stroke had affected her right arm and she was having difficulty stapling the copies, scarcely managing one for every three I was doing.

Perhaps she wasn't admitting her alcoholism, or acknow-ledging that she had hurt her daughter, but she was laboriously trying, with her poorly functioning arm, to help me staple the mountain of syllabi. When she smiled and held out the few she had stapled, I felt a tug at my heart, yet also the hopelessness of ever getting her to understand what she had done. But at least I was finally able to pray for God to forgive my mother.

9. Two Adjustments and a Diagnosis

Adjustment, in psychology, the behavioral process by which humans and other animals maintain an equilibrium among their various needs or between their needs and the obstacles of their environments.

Encyclopædia Britannica

As my two-year contract at the University of Louisville ultimately turned into a decade, my yearly schedule took on a pattern. In August, Tom and I drove to Louisville, where he would help me begin the semester, then fly back to Austin after a month. The first few years I flew to Austin for both Thanksgiving and Christmas, with a flight back to Louisville in between. We were fortunate that Tom's being self employed allowed him the freedom to work online from any location.

This routine proved too exhausting, so Tom began to fly to Louisville for Thanksgiving, stayed to help me wind up the fall semester and then we'd fly back to Austin together for Christmas. In April Tom would fly to Louisville, stay for a month to help me end the semester and pack for the drive home to Austin for the summer. This way, we were together almost seven months a year, frequent phone calls and emails bridging the five apart.

Every Christmas we visited Mother in Dallas, often while my brother and his wife took a brief vacation. This time away became more important for them as Mother's health declined. They lived only a block away and provided more of her care as her age advanced.

I was grateful that they had taken on the task of caring for her. Given my unresolved feelings and the way Mother's voice and behavior triggered memories of the years of psychiatric abuse, I knew I could never have become her caregiver. I was also grateful that I had a ready excuse: a job far away.

As Mother's health declined, there were more minor strokes, then several falls around the house, and some evidence of cognitive decline as well. By her ninety-second birthday, it was clear that a better solution was needed. My brother and sister-in-law coped heroically with hospitalizations, strokes, infections, and rehab placement. Tom and I were able to visit in January at the rehab center where Mother was recovering from what the doctors suspected had been a stroke or series of small ones. She was suspicious and defensive and, always independent, kept getting up from bed without calling for help. She fell several more times.

On the plane, I prayed to the Holy Spirit to give me the right words to help my mother. At the rehab center, Mother recognized both me and Tom, who had driven up from Austin. She could converse logically, but it was obvious that she did not completely comprehend where she was and why. At one point one of the nurse's aides, a young woman in her twenties, asked her, "Do you like to read?" Suspicious of her intent, Mother told me after the aide left the room, "They're just trying to see if I'm crazy."

I tried to allay her fears. "Mother," I said carefully, "you have been very disoriented for a couple of weeks; the doctors think you may have had another stroke." She seemed to grasp this information with gratitude, finally understanding what was going on. The word she had heard prior to my use of *disoriented* had been *confused*. My brother, his wife, and the health aides had been telling her, "You have been confused," yet *confused* was a word she associated with mental illness. I thanked God for helping me find the right words, in this case a single word, to help my mother.

After placement in an assisted living center did not work out because of more obvious cognitive decline, Mother endured another hospitalization for infections and disorientation, and her doctor, my brother, and I made the difficult decision to let nature take its course in hospice care. My brother and sister-in-law scrambled to find an appropriate facility, and this was the last place I saw her.

In April Tom and I flew down to Dallas for what we knew was probably the last time we would see her alive. I was glad

Mother's pain seemed well controlled and that my brother was taking good care of her. Although she tried to speak, she could form no intelligible words. She seemed to recognize me and lifted her hand from the bed to grasp mine, trying to say something to me. I stayed in the room with her for some time, telling her of the dogwoods beginning to bloom in Louisville, just as they had so many springtimes in Birmingham. I told her I forgave her – not because I actually felt that I had finally forgiven her, but because I thought this was what she needed to hear.

On April 28, the day before I was to give my last final exam, my brother called to tell us Mother had died. The hospice nurse who had been with her said that it had been a peaceful death, that as she exhaled for the last time, her hands unclenched, and then she did not breathe in again.

A few days later, after I gave my last final exams, Tom and I drove home to Austin, and then turned around and drove to Dallas for Mother's memorial service at the Presbyterian church where Christa had served. My aunt and cousins from Ballinger came. One of the cousins from California made the trip; Mother's second brother and his wife were too ill to take the flight. Dad's youngest sister and her son also arrived from Oklahoma. I felt awkward among these family members. The familiar feelings of not knowing what they had been told about me, of the stigma of the label applied to me as a teenager, contributed to my un-easiness about not knowing what the others were really thinking about me.

I was glad that I had read Erving Goffman's ideas on how stigma affects individuals and thus had a way to understand my awkwardness: "The stigmatized individual," Goffman writes, "may find that he feels unsure of how we normals will identify him and receive him."[58]

I felt self-conscious of my tears during the service, and angry at my brother's eulogy as well as the minister's reading of Mother's obituary, listing her extensive travels, her advanced university degree, her twenty years of teaching, her success at directing large bridge tournaments and earning the status of Life

Master in duplicate bridge. Measured against the pain she had caused me, this list of her accomplishments was disturbing. I was afraid my tears of anger would be recognized, not simply seen as tears of grief. My awkwardness continued at the lunch at Mother's condo that my brother and his wife had carefully arranged. Fortunately, Elizabeth was there, so at least one family member besides Tom was present who knew and believed my story.

My brother suggested that Tom and I take a box of Mother's letters and other papers down to Austin to read, and during the next few weeks, I read through them all. Many of the letters were troubling, some quite so, especially one Mother had written to my brother and Grandma that contained Mother's account of the visit she and Irini had made to Houston in 1973. Mother's story differed greatly from what Irini had told me. As Mother wrote it, I had told her I wanted Irini to leave and had behaved very differently from what Irini and I both remember.

I found a carefully folded letter I had written when I was seven, the first year after Grandpa died. The delivery address was a single sentence: "Take this to heaven."

Inside, a folded piece of lined notebook paper revealed the words "I love you" twice as the folds were opened.

The "letter" itself, in my seven-year-old's printing, read:

> I love you Grandfather.
> I love you
> I love you
> I love you
> I love you
> I love you
> I love you
> I love you
> I love you
> I love you
> Love, Julia

I relived the devastating grief I had felt as a child upon losing the only adult who seemed to really care about me. Now, as an adult myself of sixty-four years, I saw through a double lens the pain of that inconsolable child.

Among the letters and papers I also found several from Grandpa to my parents, and even one card from him to me. One of his letters from 1948 when I was only a year old ended with "P.S. Kiss the babies for me." Several letters, including one from Grandma, discussed at length plans for the trip we had made to the West Coast in 1952 when I was four. Apparently they were considering leaving me with my father's parents, but in one letter Grandpa wrote, "I am sure Julia will be all right on the trip, as to the extra cost, let's don't worry about that whatever it is, it is worth it to me." In another he said, "I don't want you to worry about the money and about Hoefflers keeping Julia, for I would like to have her along. I would not go at all if one of my grandchildren did not go and two make it so much the better."

And best of all for my memory of him, Grandma wrote in one letter, "He is raving about how it is going to hurt him to have Julia cry when we leave her and how much he'd enjoy having her along." I wish I could remember more about him, particularly what his voice sounded like. But I am grateful for what memories I do have of his love for me and for the miraculous dream.

Reading through the letters and other papers Mother had kept so long allowed me time for reflection. On the internet I found a reference in a journal of mathematics citing one of her duplicate bridge algorithms as the only example ever published of a particularly complicated mathematical model.[59] Bridge was the only outlet she had for her mathematical talents. She once told me that if she had been born in my generation, she would have loved to study computer systems, another reason beyond the financial for persuading me to do the same.

A strong and intelligent person, she must have felt confined by the roles of housewife and teacher, all the while yearning for more meaningful achievement. She was good to her birth family, helping her younger brothers and contributing a large share of time and financial support to the care of her own mother.

Uncomfortable with almost any expression of strong emotion, she felt too threatened ever to address the extent of the damage done to me. Yet her many visits to Houston and later to Austin, I slowly realized, were not clumsy attempts to intrude, but motivated by a basic concern. She too in some sense had been victimized by Larkin and a psychiatric system all too willing to pathologize normal feelings and behavior.

I remembered that Mother had completed a commonly used personality inventory as an entry point to counseling with Christa. She had learned her "type" and Christa had spoken with her about the various types and their characteristics, and how each communicates best. Mother's type was notably different from mine, and Mother seemed finally to grasp something significant. "I thought everyone was like me," she had said, in a sad, reflective voice. I wished there had been more time for her to learn and heal, to engage in her own search for truth.

After dealing with Mother's papers and letters, I realized many questions about Larkin remained unanswered. Was there any record of his being fired from the hospital? What had happened to him afterwards? Had he continued to practice medicine somewhere?

From various internet searches, I discovered that he had obtained a license to practice medicine in Texas in 1976, making me wonder if that had indeed been Larkin I had seen in Alfred's Deli that day with Karl.

In Larkin's obituary in the *Huntsville Times* there was no mention of his position at the private mental hospital, where at one point he had been advanced to clinical director. There was also no mention of his serving on the faculty of the University Medical School in Birmingham. All that was included about his Birmingham years was that he had a private practice there for twenty years before moving to Huntsville.

This information spurred me on to search for the elusive newspaper article Irini had mentioned. On the way to Louisville, Tom and I stopped for a few days' visit with Despina and Irini in Birmingham. While we were there, we combed through microfilmed telephone directories at the library. We found that Larkin no longer practiced at the private hospital after 1973. In the 1974 phone books he was listed as practicing from his Birmingham home address. In the 1975 phone books his name was not included in the list of practicing physicians.

Heading on toward Louisville, we drove to Huntsville and checked the telephone books there as well, finding similar evidence: an office address was listed beginning in 1977. The National Directory of Medical Specialists showed the same Birmingham residence address for the years 1974 through 1983, but each year included a note indicating that the address could not be verified, meaning that Larkin had not sent in an update for nine years. Then in 1984, he was listed as teaching family practice medicine in Huntsville. This confusing information suggested to me that something suspicious had occurred.

During the fall semester, I spoke again with my aunt in Ballinger, who told me she had never understood why my mother had me shocked and put me in a mental hospital. "You always seemed like a normal teenager to me," she said.

I pursued the matter of the Birmingham newspaper article, ordering microfilms through the University's interlibrary loan and searching diligently several years' worth of newspapers. This was tedious work, but I was determined to find the article. I berated myself for not beginning the search long before. Unfortunately, Irini couldn't remember the exact year she had read the article. Her closest estimate was that it had appeared sometime between 1976 and about 1979. That was a lot of microfilms to get through!

I also learned something new in a phone call with Aunt Elizabeth, my dad's youngest sister. When I was around seven or eight, her sister, my Aunt Eleanor, had told her about something she had heard me say when Eleanor, my mother, and I were visiting one of the great aunts in Texas.

Great Aunt Maude was a sweet lady who doted on children and I loved visiting her. She had a large cardboard box filled with beautiful buttons that she and I would play with, sitting together on the floor, exclaiming over the different kinds and colors as if they were a cask of jewels.

Eleanor, Elizabeth told me, had been quite disturbed when she heard me ask Aunt Maude, "Do you want a little girl?"

I emailed my friend Beverly about this. "That is so, so sad!" Beverly replied. "If I heard those words from someone younger than twelve or fourteen, it would sound like a cannon going off." It was validating, even after all those years, to know that someone, anyone, had noticed our family dynamics and was concerned about me.

I also recalled a strange incident, which I related to Aunt Elizabeth over the phone. Once when I was visiting in Birmingham before Tom and I were married, Mother and I were taking a book to one of her bridge friends in a neighborhood I wasn't familiar with. I saw a house with the name Larkin on the mailbox. "Look, do you think that is where Larkin lives?" I said. "No, he retired or moved away or something," she said slowly, with an elaborate shrug, pursing her lips and looking straight ahead. Mother must have known more than she disclosed about Larkin's leaving Birmingham.

As I gathered evidence and reconstructed events and facts, my quest began to resemble a detective story. And I was indeed attempting to solve a mystery. But the true goal of the quest was to integrate my memories and whatever evidence – hospital records, letters, memories of other family members and friends, information about PTSD and family systems therapy – into a coherent whole that made sense of what had happened to me. This was my own story, not Larkin's or my mother's or what others might have thought. As I reconnected with my aunts and friends and discussed these things with them as well as with new friends, therapists, and clergy, I began to feel I was no longer separated by the fear of stigma, but part of a larger community who had interceded for me, who had come into the circle one by one and led me back to the world.

Although I was enjoying teaching my graduate seminars and undergraduate classes and felt that I was making a valuable contribution to my students' education, I decided it was time to retire from the University. In February of 2011, my tenth year, I turned in my resignation to the dean of the music school at Louisville. That May, Tom and I made the last trip home to Austin after giving away most of my Louisville furniture – inexpensive bookshelves, sofa, and folding tables – to my graduate students, who were glad to come pick up the items. We stopped once more in Birmingham and looked through more microfilms, again with no luck in finding the article. But it was good to visit with Irini and Despina again.

When we reached Austin from the last trip home from Louisville, another adjustment – to retirement – began. Arriving home, unpacking books and papers, and setting up the furniture the movers had delivered occupied several weeks, and I worked slowly, trying to pick up the threads of my life in Austin, trying to adjust to whatever retirement would bring.

I taught one semester at Texas State University, subbing for a professor on medical leave, and used my brief faculty affiliation to request microfilms from Birmingham, but still had no luck in the search for the article. I requested microfilms of the newspapers from the public libraries, but discovered the only way to acquire them through interlibrary loan was through an academic research library. Since I was no longer affiliated with a university, this avenue of research was closed to me. During several visits with Despina and Irini in Birmingham, Tom and I searched through more microfilms at the library. We had no luck finding the article.

I thought more about my experiences with Larkin and why they still troubled me. I sought out books that might help me understand the impasse of justice and forgiveness, and came across Miroslav Volf's *The End of Memory: Remembering Rightly in a Violent World*. Volf's words came as a revelation to me, a perfect articulation of my dilemma:

> *If no one remembers a misdeed or names it publicly, it remains invisible. To the outside observer, its victim is not a victim, and its perpetrator is not a perpetrator; both are misperceived because the*

suffering of the one and the violence of the other go unseen – the first when the original deed is done and the second when it disappears. This injustice of hiding wrongs fuels the strong urge many victims feel to make known what they have suffered, even if some are hesitant to speak up. Since the public remembering of wrongs is an act that acknowledges them, it is therefore also an act of justice. This holds true at both the personal and broader levels.[60]

After finishing Volf's book, I decided it was time to go at least partially public about my experiences and posted under a pseudonym on several websites for survivors of psychiatric abuse. Each time I posted, I requested a reply from anyone knowing anything about Larkin.

One post brought a response from a man in Birmingham who had endured shock treatments as a young teenager several years after I did at the same private hospital. He was the one who told me that another psychiatrist who practiced there had appeared on a local television talk show exposing the overuse of electroshock at the hospital.

I contacted the television station hoping that they might still have a tape of the interview, but they replied that live local shows from that time were not archived. I wrote letters to each of the psychiatrist's two daughters praising their father's initiative and asking if they could provide any further information, but I never received a reply. Every lead seemed to be turning into a dead end.

Resolved to continue my search for the article, I asked my former University of Texas piano teacher if she would allow me to be listed as a proxy on her interlibrary loan account. Claire generously gave her permission and I was all set to begin the process, when health issues began to intervene.

In March of 2013 I began to experience dental pain and a strange numbness in my chin. Our dentist saw the need for a root canal and began the process, but the root canal did not help the problem. Three teeth eventually had to be pulled, revealing a suspicious area in the jaw. The dentist biopsied the area and sent the sample to a pathologist.

On May 20, 2013, Tom let me sleep as long as possible and then gently woke me to tell me that the pathologist had called to say that the biopsy confirmed a diagnosis of lymphoma.

10. Triggers and Cancer Treatment

When in danger, it's natural to feel afraid. This fear triggers many split-second changes in the body to prepare to defend against the danger or to avoid it. This "fight-or-flight" response is a healthy reaction meant to protect a person from harm. But in post-traumatic stress disorder (PTSD), this reaction is changed or damaged. People who have PTSD may feel stressed or frightened even when they're no longer in danger. [61]

Secondary wounding [in PTSD] occurs by responding negatively to the survivor's account of the trauma, the magnitude of its aftereffects, the meaning to the survivor, or its impact on the survivor's life. ... The reactions survivors have to triggers, along with trying to cope with PTSD symptoms, can inflame negative reactions from others. These moments ... can leave survivors feeling stigmatized. It is very important to realize that regardless of other people's ignorance or insensitivity, survivors are entitled to their response to the trigger. [62]

– Annemarie Huppert

After the initial diagnosis of cancer, Tom and I were at a loss. Our neighbor Doris, a retired oncology nurse, urged us to contact a doctor as soon as possible. I called a friend from graduate school whose husband was an oncologist at MD Anderson in Houston, but getting an appointment there would take time, she said. So we made an appointment with our family practice physician, who recommended an oncologist in Austin.

Our days then became a confusing round of tests, consultations, blood draws, and frightening discoveries about ports and catheters. There were printed handouts about chemotherapy detailing painful and sometimes debilitating side effects. The new language Tom and I had to learn about the disease, drugs, and procedures was a challenge, but we tried to master its vocabulary quickly.

Understanding my history, the Austin oncologist prescribed anti-anxiety medication I could take before any procedure that might evoke the trauma of nearly fifty years ago. After a series of tests, I received a phone call from MD Anderson that I had an appointment for June 3.

At my first appointment in Houston, the nurse had scarcely started to take my blood pressure when I began to tremble and cry. I covered my face with my hands. "Look at me! Look at me!" the nurse repeated, as one might calm a child. Waiting in the hall after hearing my name called had triggered responses suppressed in Larkin's office before each electroshock. Now that I no longer needed to suppress them, even when I tried, I couldn't.

The nurse left the room for a few minutes. When she return-ed, I managed to explain my past experience of medical trauma. "These are ethical doctors," she reassured me, and continued the intake. She brought Tom from the waiting room, who quietly held my hand. When the doctor arrived, she examined me and ordered a battery of tests. I told her more of my history and she seemed to understand.

PTSD triggers were something I had to deal with often during these cancer tests and procedures. Part of a group of symptoms classified as "intrusion symptoms," triggers are reminders of the traumatic event that cause distress in the person experiencing them. Dreams, flashbacks, or simple memories can be other symptoms with this intrusive, unwelcome nature. Particularly distressing are sudden dissociative reactions or flashbacks, where a PTSD sufferer may feel or act as if the trauma is happening again.[63] Even an object, a person, or a place can trigger or bring up painful memories of trauma.

Over the next ten days, I didn't know when, how, or to what degree I might react to any test or procedure. Having to lie down for tests and scans. Feeling the needles go into my arm or hand to draw blood or infuse contrast chemicals for the scans. Undergoing anesthesia for a bone marrow biopsy. Being asked many questions about my medical history. Not knowing how long the complete protocol would take or what it would do to me. All of these could trigger the traumatic events I experienced under Larkin's misguided regimen.

I took the anti-anxiety medication the Austin oncologist had prescribed, yet often during these initial cancer tests I would feel a rising panic as something, anything, would evoke the past. When I was trapped in the mental hospital or awaiting yet another outpatient shock, an involuntary process had numbed my responses to the overwhelming fear. I could not complain, could not cry, if only to keep from giving Larkin a reason to cause me more pain. Now that I was fully conscious of that process, however, I could only try to endure the fear fully aware.

I would become angry – the fight response, which I suppressed as quickly as I could, but not always successfully. I would start to choke up to keep from crying. My shoulders and arms would tense and, just as I had done years ago in Birmingham, I would find myself holding my breath to keep from expressing my anger. The doctors and staff at MD Anderson would be uncomfortable and I more vulnerable and ashamed.

I somehow made it through the days of tests in a constant struggle with the heightened sensitivity typical of PTSD, sometimes crying inappropriately, and more rarely making angry remarks to staff or doctors, but always tense and always afraid. If an angry tone of voice slipped out, I instantly became even more tense, as if guarding against a blow, afraid they would judge me or hurt me in some way. At least this time I knew they were not going to give me shock treatments. Yet the feeling of fear embedded in these memories, irrational though it was, kept surfacing, no matter how much I tried to suppress or calm it.

It is impossible for someone who hasn't experienced it to understand that no amount of will power or "positive thinking" can stop these kinds of reactions when a similar trigger occurs. This was especially true for feelings I could not quickly escape by leaving the room or in this case leaving the hospital and refusing truly life-saving treatment.

Before we left for home, we were told that the initial diagnosis had been refined to something more serious: an intermediate kind of lymphoma, somewhere between diffuse large B-cell and Burkitt's lymphoma. This meant that the chemotherapy had to be particularly strong, with continuous infusions during six five-day inpatient hospitalizations, each separated only by a couple of weeks.[64]

Back in Austin, I was scheduled for six rounds of inpatient chemotherapy at St. David's South, where a surgeon implanted a port beneath the skin. The port was defective: destructive chemotherapy drugs were leaking into my skin and muscle. The large, slowly spreading chemical burn required surgical removal of the port and many visits to the wound care clinic, while the chemotherapy itself slowed down the healing. A constant source of pain and concern over the next eight months, the wound made me even more vulnerable to stress and triggers than I might have been otherwise.

On the next trip down to MD Anderson, the doctor told us my PET/CT scans showed that the disease was responding well. But the diagnosis had been narrowed yet again to an even more serious form of lymphoma: "double hit lymphoma," in which two genes become misaligned, increasing the cancer's aggressiveness.

The only hope for a cure was a stem cell transplant. This meant the addition of two rounds of more intense, high-dose chemotherapy in two hospital stays, the second of which could last up to a month or more. It also meant that we would have to relocate to Houston for three months.[65] When I heard all this in the doctor's office, I couldn't hold back the tears.

With what had already happened after the initial diagnosis and preliminary tests in Austin, I realized I would need help facing the more difficult procedures and long hospital stays the transplant would mean for me. I had noticed in a brochure that MD Anderson offered counseling and therapy for patients needing help dealing with cancer diagnosis and treatment. Before we returned to Austin, I contacted the coordinator and requested a referral to one of their counselors.

Three weeks later we were back in Houston for more procedures to test my health status prior to the stem cell transplant.

In the doctor's office after one series of tests, I was anxious and uncomfortable. I must have made the doctor uneasy as well, for she told me that I might not be allowed to have a transplant if I didn't first pass a psychiatric review "to be sure I could handle it." This was the same doctor who just three weeks earlier had told me the only hope for a cure was a stem cell transplant.

I felt forced into an all too familiar power game. While Larkin had been destroying me with a harrowing treatment I did not need, this woman was threatening to withhold a treatment that could save my life.

Afterwards I told myself that the doctor might have just come from the bedside of a patient much worse off than I, and I should be grateful that the transplant had a good chance of curing me. Caught up in the professional task of giving a patient important information, the doctor could only deal with my fears as an inconvenient impediment to telling me what I needed to know.

After enduring six rounds of chemotherapy, we relocated to Houston at the end of October for the three-month stay, having found an apartment offered by a church group at a special rate for MD Anderson patients. The first couple of days there were several orientation sessions for new stem cell patients as well as more procedures to undergo. I found out they had scheduled me to see a psychiatrist instead of a counselor.

At first the psychiatrist was quite gracious. He agreed that in the 1960s I had been treated egregiously, in a way that made him "ashamed of the profession." I was relieved he was taking my concerns seriously. He had helpful advice on how to communicate with doctors uncomfortable with patients who cry: "Tell them you can listen or talk even if you're crying." His diagnosis was twofold: post-traumatic stress disorder and, as one would expect, adjustment issues related to the diagnosis of cancer.

Subsequent meetings, however, did not go as well. He seemed interested primarily in having a means to control me should I become psychotic, a side effect known to occur from the chemotherapy for which I was scheduled.[66] I could understand this concern, but the thought of being dosed with Haldol – a strong psychotropic drug – through an IV against my wishes was not something I relished.

Taking issue with my advance directive as I had written it, he requested that I change it to allow the administration of psychotropic drugs if deemed necessary. I did change the directive, but included the stipulation that these classes of drugs could only be used with the express permission of the person holding my medical power of attorney, my husband, Tom.

Before the first two PET/CT scans there was enough time for the anti-anxiety medicine prescribed by the Austin oncologist to take effect. For the third, however, Tom and I arrived half an hour early for the appointment, expecting to wait, but my name was called and they wanted me to begin immediately.

Before the actual scan the patient is installed in a reclining chair in a little cubicle and injected through an IV with a small amount of radioactive substance which concentrates in the location of the cancer and thus pinpoints its location on the scan. After the IV is removed, the patient is to sit alone quietly for an hour or more and not read, listen to music, or talk to anyone while the substance circulates throughout the body. There were many of these thin-walled cubicles all in a row and each one usually occupied – they do dozens of PET/CT scans every day.

A few minutes after the technician gave me the injection, my breathing became rapid and shallow. I began to cry, but tried to hold back the tears, which only made my breathing more ragged. He returned to the cubicle and asked me if he could help; I was cold, so he brought more blankets. By the time he came back again I was sobbing. "Could you please keep it down so the other patients don't think we're torturing you?" he asked kindly. I smiled faintly, appreciating his humor. I asked if he could hold my hand, yet still my crying would not stop.

During the wait in the small cubicle, I was afraid I would die of cancer. I was afraid of the whole process of the stem cell transplant. And I was even more afraid that they would keep on treating me and treating me with ever more painful and difficult treatments, without regard for my life becoming nothing but torture. I was afraid I would eventually die, but not before they had tortured me continually for a long time in the name of curing me of cancer. Just like Larkin was supposedly battling a mental illness, rooting it out of my brain with no regard for me as a person, not even enough regard to see the obvious – that I was not mentally ill, but that my parents had major problems with honesty and alcohol and bitterness.

I told the tech guy I had taken the anti-anxiety medicine right before, but it had not yet taken effect. He said it probably would in a few more minutes. I must have been sobbing for at least half an hour of the time the patient is to be calm when the anti-anxiety medicine finally began to work. When I lay down in the machine for the PET/CT scan, I fell asleep.

The next day at an appointment with the physician's assistant for the stem cell doctor, the PA asked me if I'd had any cosmetic treatments on my eyes recently. She said that the PET scan was completely clear except for some new activity around the eyes, but it didn't look like lymphoma. I laughed and told her what had happened. "Yes," she said, "crying would have caused it."

She said the machines were so sensitive they could pick up any activity of a patient in the hour before the scan. In the early days of PET scans patients watched television while they were supposed to be waiting calmly, but this caused the scans to show activity in the eyes and brain.

At a later appointment, another PA told me they had all been mystified as to what the activity around my eyes had meant. It was obviously not lymphoma, but it was definitely something. We laughed at this point, and she said the next time if they called my name too early for the injection I was to tell them I had to stay in the waiting room until the anti-anxiety medicine took effect.

This was a moment of relief, to be able to laugh with the PAs and learn interesting facts about the complicated tests and machines. The scan was not ruined; it still showed no recurrence of lymphoma. And figuring out with the PAs why the activity around the eyes had appeared allowed me to see the medical staff as people who were not causing me pain or judging me because I had cried during the procedure.

I'm sure I was not the best patient, and the medical staff had to take extra care to help me. I was grateful that they understood I was dealing, in a sense, with dual realities: the immediate reality of cancer tests and treatment and the medical trauma forty years ago those procedures brought to the surface.

It took me several days to understand what had been the PTSD trigger in the PET scan process. First, of course, the anti-anxiety medicine had not had time to take effect. But in a telephone conversation with my friend Jocelynn, I realized the actual trigger was neither the earlier electroshocks nor the PET scan machine. It was waiting in the small PET cubicle that triggered the thoughts and feelings I experienced while having to endure the long wait in the basement room of the outpatient clinic thirty-five times from 1966 through 1969.

Talking through all of this with Jocelynn after the PET scan, I came up with a plan for processing each trigger. My theory was that each one needed to be understood, processed, and grieved. It was important to pin down what the exact trigger was and what response it triggered. Helping me process each trigger involved talking with a close friend about the trigger and its cause. Each one also caused some emotional reaction, and my friends listened and validated my reactions to each trigger as I grieved the original trauma that had evoked it.

Many of the procedures were triggering. Inserting a catheter to replace the failed port was painful, especially since the pre-medication, a liquid form of the sedative Versed, didn't work. The doctor did not inject enough local anesthetic; the incisions felt like razor cuts. I cried throughout the procedure, unable to suppress my emotional responses to both past and present hurts. I came to understand that the reason I cried so much during these cancer testing procedures was intertwined with having had to repress any show of emotion before or after each electroshock to avoid the punishment of more. I was crying for fear of both present and past medical treatments.

Another problem with the psychiatrist arose as I was trying to explain how this procedure had been a trigger. I mentioned in passing that oral Versed had been used as a pre-medication.

"There is no such thing as oral Versed," he interrupted.

"Oh, I thought that was what they said it was – a vile tasting pink liquid," I said, rather than argue the point. "They gave me two doses to drink, but maybe I was wrong." I began to doubt that I wanted to see him again.

When we were discussing the difficulties of a stem cell transplant, the psychiatrist said, "It is beyond anything you can possibly imagine." I had just been telling him how frightened I was of the high dose chemotherapy and the transplant. Why on earth was he trying to make me even more afraid?

I also tried to explain how important it was to find the newspaper article about Larkin's discipline by the state board so I could post it on the internet along with my experience. "Well, why don't you just post your story on the web without the article?" he asked.

That evening Tom helped me articulate the reason finding the article was so important. Without the article, I would be just one more former mental patient complaining about how I had been treated – there would be no external evidence of Larkin's malpractice. Recognizing the psychiatrist's dismissive response as secondary wounding, I became more certain that I did not want to meet with him again. I sent an email cancelling the next appointment.

Perhaps I couldn't extend much trust to any psychiatrist, and if I had continued seeing this man I might have come to trust him, but my experience of Larkin had obviously colored my feelings. I felt strongly that I should not have to work with someone I couldn't trust, and I had the right to stop meeting with him, a right I never had as a teenager forced into needless electroshock and a debilitating hospitalization.

Navigating the triggers became easier as I talked through each one with Tom or on the telephone with Jocelynn or Beverly. I came to understand how each related to previous experiences with Larkin's treatment. Some of the triggers were general ones and thus more difficult to identify readily – the uncertainty of how long each step of the process would take, for example.

Stem cell collection took seven sessions, while most people's bodies yield plenty of stem cells in three or four.[67] Lying on my back for the various procedures – PET scans, MRIs, echocardiograms, transfusions – was also a trigger, although this became easier as I met more nurses and techs who were compassionate, competent, and forthcoming about each procedure.

For the most part, the stem cell protocol was significantly different from my experience of Larkin. The nurses explained to me that I had the right to refuse any drug, and to ask what each drug was and what its side effects might be. The treatment itself had its elements of pain and embarrassment, but the nurses were all efficient and competent, concerned and respectful. Unlike the mystery of what Larkin wrote about me as his patient or surmised from my mother's "monitoring," the results of all tests, blood work, and even patient reports about me were available for me to read on the MD Anderson secure website.

After checking in to the inpatient stem cell unit on December 23, for a week I underwent the high dose chemotherapy regimen that prepared my body for the actual transplant. As difficult as it was to be in the hospital over Christmas, the nurses helped keep our spirits up. One of the nurses wore a funny headband of cloth reindeer antlers, and another showed me how to find the music channels on the television so I could listen to Christmas music. With our friend Karl in Germany, I had long conversations over Skype, reminiscing about our time in Houston in the 1970s. The Christmas cards Tom and I placed on the windowsill helped lend some cheer, and on my prescribed daily walks I enjoyed seeing the Christmas decorations on the unit.

On the day of the transplant, December 30, two nurses certified in the details were required to stay by the bedside during the entire two hours of the infusion. Tom and I had asked a hospital chaplain to bless the stem cells and the process, and

Pastor David came to my room. He said a beautiful prayer for "new life" and led Tom, me, and the two nurses in the Lord's Prayer. Later that afternoon he came back and celebrated communion with Tom and me.

The transplant went well, said the stem-cell doctors during daily bedside rounds. The first week the side effects were rough, but the nurses addressed pain control quickly and efficiently. During these slow days, I was grateful the music therapy department had arranged to let me have a portable electronic keyboard in my hospital room. I even used it to write a song, "Come Back Stem Cells," to the tune of the 1962 hit by The Lettermen, "Come Back Silly Girl,"[68] and sang it for the nurses.

Tom was with me the better part of each day, always patient and helpful. When I couldn't eat anything on the hospital menu, he brought wonton soup from our favorite Houston restaurant.

After twenty-two long days in the inpatient stem cell unit, I was discharged to the Houston apartment Tom and I had rented. We remained in Houston another three weeks, visiting the stem cell clinic every few days for blood counts, transfusions, infusions, shots, and monitoring to be sure nothing was going wrong.

On February 5, the stem cell doctor said I could return to Austin, and after Beverly arrived from Washington, DC, Tom left to take the first load of stuff home so he would be there for the house to be cleaned as advised by the protocols for preventing infection.

The next day, Beverly and I left for Austin in the car she had rented at the Houston airport. Because I began running a fever, it was touch and go the night before our departure. The fever was down to normal in the morning, so we took off for the drive home.[69] A long recovery lay ahead, with many trips to Houston required in the next months and years for scans and checkups, but for now I was going home, on a road trip with my friend since fourth grade.

11. NEW BEGINNINGS

To assist another is to do God's work. To redeem one person is to redeem the world.[70]

–Rabbi Isaac Luria

Doubtless, others in my extended family would disbelieve what I have written here or argue that things happened differently. Yet they were not present when many of the events described in this book occurred. Most likely they will never read this memoir unless they stumble across it on the internet.

As of summer 2014 I was declared in remission with no evidence of disease on the PET and CT scans or in the bone marrow. My blood counts, however, have not recovered as they should, and weekly testing continues, showing a slow improvement. The road ahead still has many obstacles – late effects, the possibility of cancer recurrence or new cancers, the slow recovery of the immune system and blood counts, immunizations for all childhood diseases, dental work to replace the missing teeth, a skin graft to heal the wound from the chemotherapy burn that keeps reopening, no air travel for at least one year, and no travel outside of the country for two.

As the events of the past year of cancer treatment begin to fade, with the slow return of my energy, and with the ongoing act of writing about my experiences of trauma, my despairing feelings about what happened in the past have lessened. I have experienced a growing hope that writing and publishing this book will reveal long hidden wrongs and function in a small way as an act of justice.

I regret that I haven't been able to find the newspaper article Irini told me about, but I will continue my search and if I do locate it, I plan to post it on the web.

With my parents both dead, I no longer experience the pain triggered when seeing them or speaking with them. This has allowed me to reflect more dispassionately on the past. I continue to pray for them to be healed and made whole.

Through the years an overarching irony has become clear to me: as someone who had grown up with alcoholic parents, I had no way to recognize how seriously compromised my mother and dad were by their drinking and the drugs they voluntarily took. And they did not recognize how seriously compromised and traumatized I was from all the drugs and electroshocks, all forced upon me against my will.

I believe that God is merciful, and that my parents were not fully aware of what they were doing. Neither would I want to see Larkin in any hell of everlasting torment. Although I believe he was fundamentally motivated by financial gain, he was probably taught in medical school that electroshock was an effective treatment for mental illness. His diagnostic skills were woefully lacking, and I suspect he made a racket of diagnosing teenagers like the girls in the ward, frightening their parents with dire predictions of their child's fate unless they gave him carte blanche to shock and drug their child. I also believe he enjoyed the prestige of a medical degree and having absolute power over his patients.

My fantasy for a judgment scene for Larkin and my parents would entail a kind of trial, but not a hostile one. The process would also include many, many hours of kind, caring people talking to them individually, helping them to heal from all the things that hurt them in their lives, and helping them to recognize and grieve over their wrongful actions that hurt themselves and others. At some point in this fantasy of healing and restorative justice, they could admit that what they did was wrong. Perhaps they could even be reconciled in a right relationship with me and with each other, as in the circle prayer at Pecos.

On the other hand, I am taking precautions to ensure that I will never be kept alive on torturous machines rather than be allowed to die. I have written a living will that includes a section on voluntarily stopping eating and drinking, and have stated in my advance directive that under no circumstances may any kind of electroshock be used, a precaution I feel necessary because today, the majority of electroshock patients are elderly women.[71] I pray every night that when death comes, God will let me die peacefully in my sleep in my own bed.

How anyone faces mortality is uniquely his or her own process, the result of personal experience and faith. In the years that remain to me I hope to contribute to the redeeming of the world, and if despair threatens, I will try to remember the miracles I have experienced in my life – the answer to my prayer to kiss and hug Grandpa one more time, the way I was guided to find Paul through the magazines my mother hid from me, and the phone call from Jim that saved my life. I will also remember the grace of finding my loving husband, the world class medical care I was privileged to receive for cancer, and the kind acts of all the people who reached out to me when I was in despair – all the beautiful friends who helped rescue me from the lion's mouth.[72]

Epilogue: The Last Word

When I was at the University of Michigan I bought a small cork-board I placed over my desk. I used it to post reminders and schedule notes as well as famous quotations or poems I particularly liked. I had this corkboard in Birmingham also, in my bedroom and later in the dormitory.

Many years later, my brother told me that my parents, when they came to the dormitory or just at home, made a note of what quotations or poems I had pinned to the corkboard and then tried to interpret my state of mind. Why they didn't just ask me about the poems I will never understand, just as I will never understand why no one in my family and none of the doctors tried to talk to me or listen to me when I tried to tell them my reasons for coming home from Michigan.

One item I remember pinning to the corkboard was "The Last Word," a poem by Matthew Arnold I had studied in English class at the University of Michigan:

Creep into thy narrow bed,
Creep, and let no more be said!
Vain thy onset! all stands fast.
Thou thyself must break at last.

Let the long contention cease!
Geese are swans, and swans are geese.
Let them have it how they will!
Thou art tired: best be still.

They out-talked thee, hissed thee, tore thee?
Better men fared thus before thee;
Fired their ringing shot and passed,
Hotly charged – and sank at last.

Charge once more, then, and be dumb!
Let the victors, when they come,
When the forts of folly fall,
Find thy body by the wall!

The Michigan professor led our class to a fairly typical analysis of the text. Arnold's subject is not war or violence, but verbal conflict – the argument as war metaphor. The speaker, or persona, of the poem uses a sarcastic tone, at first suggesting that the person addressed, perhaps himself, should give up and accept defeat. But the third stanza marks a turning point, giving an example of action as opposed to talk. The fourth stanza admonishes the person addressed to act also, to continue the argument against the "forts of folly" even though it may not be until after death that the argument can be won by others.

After returning to Birmingham, I re-interpreted the poem as a personal allegory. The "narrow bed" in the first stanza was the gurney or the hospital bed. The advice to "be still" and "let them have it how they will" was the temptation to give up and accept Larkin's and my parents' image of me, to acquiesce that geese and swans are the same. The "charge" mentioned in the third stanza was the determination to make yet another attempt to convince my parents and Larkin of my sanity, one more attempt to find someone to talk with me, one more protest against the electro-shocks.

The final stanza pointed to the seriousness of the matter. This was a life or death struggle, and I could not give up or accept their view of me, which I knew to be wrong. I read this poem repeatedly, and recited it from memory to strengthen my resistance to what they were doing to me. The poem was one more means I used to stay alive and retain my identity and sanity while facing the repeated assaults of the shocks.

Today, more than fifty years later, I can still recite the poem from memory, and it still calls forth strong emotions. By writing this memoir I have attempted to have the "last word" in a larger context. I hope that my action – writing this book – can contribute to the humanizing of the mental health system and perhaps help someone else escape its folly.

NOTES

Note to Preface

1. Azar Nafisi, *Reading Lolita in Tehran: A Memoir in Books* (Random House Reissue Edition, 2008), 41.

Notes to Prologue: Families

2. The text of President Kennedy's September 7, 1961 address, along with the entire September 15, 1961 issue of *Life Magazine* containing a lengthy article "How You Can Survive Fallout" is available at http://tinyurl .com/ouvbxtt. Another essay on fallout shelters appears at http://tinyurl .com/yf3kef8.

3. F. López-Muñoz, and C. Alamo "Monoaminergic Neurotransmission: The History of the Discovery of Antidepressants from 1950s until Today," *Current Pharmaceutical Design* 15 (2009): 1563-86. The antidepressant was Nardil, a drug of the MAO inhibitor class prescribed beginning in the 1950s. Tricyclic antidepressants were not widely prescribed until the 1960s, while SSRIs (serotonin-sparing reuptake inhibitors) made their debut only in 1987, with Prozac.

4. Sarah Allen Benton, *Understanding the High-Functioning Alcoholic: Professional Views and Personal Insights* (Greenwood Publishing Group, 2009) and Buddy T., "What is a Functional Alcoholic?" updated May 22, 2014, http://goo.gl/6zt4MC (accessed September 18, 2014). The concept of the high-functioning alcoholic was not recognized for many years.

Notes to Chapter 1. Adolescence

5. Jeffrey Kluger, "The Spillover Effect: Beware the Explosive Teen" *Time,* Oct. 10, 2011, http://goo.gl/jepByY (accessed September 6, 2014).

6. Karen W. Ruebush, The Mother-Daughter Relationship and Psychological Separation in Adolescence, *Journal of Research on Adolescence* 4 (1994): 439-451, abstract available at http://www.tandfonline. com/doi/abs/10.1207/s15327795jra0403_5#preview (accessed September 6, 2014). For more on the process of adolescent separation, see Nancy Chodorow, *The Reproduction of Mothering: Psychoanalysis and the Sociology of Gender* (University of California Press, 1978) and The Menniger Clinic's brief article, "Why Are Mother/Daughter Relationships

So Difficult?" Tuesday, January 21, 2014, http://goo.gl/2n9jK4 (accessed September 6, 2014).

7. Delayed sleep phase disorder is relatively common in adolescents, but had not yet been defined in the 1960s. See Cleveland Clinic, "Delayed Sleep Phase Syndrome," http://goo.gl/GZzoJE (accessed September 6, 2014).

8. Owen Jander, "Beethoven's 'Orpheus in Hades': The Andante con Moto of the Fourth Piano Concerto," *Nineteenth Century Music* 8 (1985): 195-212.

Notes to Chapter 2. Trauma

9. Esther Giller, "What is Psychological Trauma?" http://goo.gl/46hzup (accessed September 6, 2014).

10. The MMPI (Minnesota Multiphasic Personality Inventory), published in 1943, was developed from responses given by married people living in the rural Midwest: Roderick D. Buchanan, "The Development of the Minnesota Multiphasic Personality Inventory," *Journal of the History of the Behavioral Sciences* 30, 2 (1994): 148–61. It was not until 1992 that a version of the test for adolescents was published, correcting some of the problems of using the test with teenagers: J. N. Butcher et al., *Minnesota Multiphasic Personality Inventory-Adolescent Version (MMPI-A): Manual for administration, scoring and interpretation* (University of Minnesota Press, 1992).

11. I obtained the hospital records in 1988; quotations from these records are transcribed verbatim.

12. That my mother blew these rather mundane teenage problems out of proportion shocks me even today. I am reminded of the case of Howard Dully, recounted in his book, *My Lobotomy* (Crown Publishers, 2007). Jeffrey Moussaieff Masson, https://jeffreymasson.wordpress.com/2011/12/12/the-many-forms-of-human-violence/ (accessed September 13, 2014), discusses psychiatric violence and calls Dully's case "perhaps the most shocking case of all." Dully, age twelve in 1960, received a lobotomy because of his stepmother's complaints that he was "unbelievably defiant," engaged in a "good deal of daydreaming," and "object[ed] to going to bed." Masson states that Dully's book "should be required reading of every psychiatrist." Two years after I was born (and one year after Dully's birth), the Nobel Prize in Physiology or Medicine of 1949 was awarded to the inventor of the lobotomy, Egas Moniz, "for his discovery of the therapeutic value of leucotomy in certain psychoses."

"Egas Moniz – Facts," http://goo.gl/2IyPdc (accessed September 13, 2014).

13. A typical apology for EST can be found at the Mayo Clinic website: http://goo.gl/6rXK0q (accessed September 6, 2014). Modified EST (EST with anesthesia) has been used in the United States since the early 1950s: John P. Malone, A. M. Blayney, "Modified Electroconvulsive Therapy," *Irish Journal of Medical Science* 27, 7 (1951): 315-323, http://tinyurl.com/o9pfdpb (accessed September 6, 2014).

14. Max Fink, "The Origins of Convulsive Therapy," *American Journal of Psychiatry* 141, 9 (1984): 1034–41, http://www.ncbi.nlm.nih.gov/pubmed/6147103 (accessed September 6, 2014), reports that in 1934 Ladislas Meduna, a Hungarian neuropsychiatrist, originated the idea of using chemically induced convulsions to treat schizophrenia. Meduna posited a "biological antagonism" between epilepsy and schizophrenia. Since in his experience epileptics rarely or never were schizophrenic, convulsions would eventually "cure" schizophrenics of their condition.

Opposed to this, the Harvard Health Newsletters, http://tinyurl.com/nyqhwnx (accessed September 6, 2014), recently summarized observational studies from 2005 to 2011 that found that "[p]eople with schizophrenia were nearly six times as likely to develop epilepsy compared with other people, while individuals with epilepsy were nearly eight times as likely to develop schizophrenia compared with other people," and suggested that "schizophrenia and epilepsy may share biological roots." Furthermore, the cited studies indicate that "factors that contribute to both disorders likely consist of some mix of genetic changes and environmental insults."

15. Peter Breggin, *Electroshock: Its Brain-Disabling Effects* (Springer Publishing, 1979), *Toxic Psychiatry* (St. Martin's Press, 1991), and *Brain-Disabling Treatments in Psychiatry: Drugs, Electroshock, and the Role of the FDA* (Springer Publishing, 1997). See also Breggin's website, www.breggin.com (accessed September 6, 2014).

16. Hans Hartelius, "Cerebral Changes Following Electrically Induced Convulsions," supplement to *Acta Psychiatrica Neurologica Scandinavica* 77 (1952), quoted in Breggin, *Toxic Psychiatry*, 197.

17. Ugo Cerletti, quoted in Edward Shorter and David Healy, *Shock Therapy: A History of Electroconvulsive Treatment in Mental Illness* (Rutgers University Press, 2012), 109.

18. WebMD, "Electroconvulsive Therapy and Other Depression Treatments," http://tinyurl.com/bzdrmr9 (accessed September 6, 2014) and

"Electroconvulsive Therapy (ECT)," http://tinyurl.com/oh3we6q (accessed September 6, 2014).

19. Diana Rose, Pete Fleischmann et al., "Patients' Perspectives on Electroconvulsive Therapy: Systematic Review," *The British Medical Journal,* 10 June, 2003, http://www.bmj.com /content/326/7403/1363 (accessed September 6, 2014). See http://www.mindfreedom.org (accessed September 6, 2014) for patient accounts and news of recent abuses of electroshock including forced outpatient electroshock in Minnesota as recently as 2010. Bonnie Burstow, "Electroshock as a Form of Violence Against Women," *Violence Against Women,* 12, 4 (2006): 372-392 and "Electroshock: The Gentlemen's Way to Batter Women," *Domestic Violence Report* 14, 2 (2009): 17-32, http://tinyurl.com/ny7ac23 (accessed September 16, 2014) notes the preponderance of women receiving EST.

20. Many medical EST accounts refer to this type of drug as a muscle relaxant, but the actual experience of the patient, should he or she remain conscious, is one of complete muscle paralysis. Since its introduction in 1951, Succinylcholine has become the most frequently used drug of this class in EST. Raj K Kalapatapu, "Electroconvulsive Therapy," http://tinyurl.com/mrh8r4h (accessed September 6, 2014), is typical. The drug is used to provide neuromuscular blockade (in lay terms, paralysis) in EST as well as in surgical procedures such as emergency tracheal intubation. It is also used during more extended surgical procedures. For more information on this drug see "Anectine," http://tinyurl.com/mw5m7p9 (accessed September 6, 2014).

21. Lists of the side effects of Chlorpromazine may be found at Inchem (International Programme on Chemical Safety), http://goo.gl/nLGiB6 (accessed September 6, 2014). For a description of the dangers of the so-called second generation of anti-psychotic drugs, see Richard A. Friedman, M.D., "A Call for Caution on Antipsychotic Drugs," *The New York Times,* September 25, 2012, http://goo.gl/qlbiJk (accessed September 6, 2014).

22. The sixteenth treatment that summer occurred on August 13, 1965, eleven days after this letter was written.

23. American Psychiatric Association, *Diagnostic and Statistical Manual of Mental Disorders, Fifth Edition: DSM-5* (American Psychiatric Association, 2013), 280-281.

24. As noted above, the convulsion caused by the application of electric current to the brain was thought to produce a "cure."

25. Anosognosia is the medical term used when a person cannot recognize an illness. A catch-22 for someone not mentally ill but wrongly diagnosed, psychiatrists may see protests that they have been misdiagnosed as anosognosia. The more a patient protests the diagnosis of mental illness, the graver the psychiatrist views the patient's condition. As Thomas Szasz recognizes in *Psychiatry: The Science of Lies* (Syracuse University Press, 2008), 3, "In the Anglo-American adversarial legal system, the accused is presumed innocent until proven otherwise, and the onus of proof of guilt is on the accuser. In the psychiatric-inquisitorial 'medical' system, this relationship is reversed: the person diagnosed as mentally ill is presumed insane until proven otherwise, and the onus of disproof of insanity is on the (usually powerless) individual incriminated as 'insane.' A priori, psychiatrists disqualify such claims of 'psychiatric innocence' as evidence of the 'insane patient's denial of his illness.'"

26. Linda Andre, *Doctors of Deception: What They Don't Want You to Know about Shock Treatment* (Rutgers University Press, 2009). Andre received electroshock in the 1980s and emerged from the hospital with five years of memory erased.

27 Albert Camus, *The Myth of Sisyphus*, quoted in Gordon Marino, ed., *Basic Writings of Existentialism* (Modern Library, 2004), 463.

28. Trauma Recovery, "Fight, Flight, Freeze Responses," http://tinyurl.com/ldt22nx (accessed September 6, 2014).

29. International Society for the Study of Trauma and Dissociation http://www.isst-d.org/default.asp?contentID=76#diss (accessed September 6, 2014) notes, "In severe forms of dissociation, disconnection occurs in the usually integrated functions of consciousness, memory, identity, or perception. For example, someone may think about an event that was tremendously upsetting, yet have no feelings about it. Clinically, this is termed emotional numbing, one of the hallmarks of post-traumatic stress disorder."

Notes to Chapter 3. ...And More Trauma

30. Bronwen Bryant and Kathleen Knights, *Pharmacology for Health Professionals,* 3rd ed. (Elsevier, Australia, 2011), http://www.the-medical-dictionary.com/thorazine.htm (accessed September 6, 2014) note "the phenothiazines are notoriously 'dirty' drugs as they antagonize receptors for dopamine, acetylcholine, noradrenaline and histamine." Oregon Health and Science University, "Dirty Drugs Have Their Day," http://goo.gl/cBMiYU (accessed September 6, 2014) discusses the ongoing

development of anti-cancer drugs, noting that researchers are re-thinking the concept of dirty drugs and beginning to view drugs that act on a number of different targets as potentially more curative for cancer.

31. Narco-analysis first came into use to treat shell shock during WWI, then combat fatigue during WWII. The idea behind the technique is that the drugs used to induce the hypnotic state disinhibit the patient from disclosing information to the psychiatrist when questioned, and that patients under narco-analysis are also susceptible to suggestions made by the psychiatrist. See John Stephen Horsely, *Narco-analysis: A new technique in short-cut psychotherapy: a comparison with other methods: and notes on the barbiturates* (Oxford University Press, 1943) for one of the earliest published books on the subject. Many references are available on the internet; see, for example, Minnu Panditrao, "Propofol for Narcoanalysis, A Novel and Better Alternative: Preliminary Report of Four Cases," *Indian Journal of Clinical Practice*, 3, 20 (2009): 256-260, http://goo.gl/M8aM98 (accessed September 6, 2014).

32. Judith Herman, *Trauma and Recovery: The Aftermath of Violence – from Domestic Abuse to Political Terror* (Basic Books, 1992), 85, asserts, "During the course of their captivity, victims frequently describe alternating between periods of submission and more active resistance. The second, irreversible stage in the breaking of a person is reached when the victim loses the will to live. This is not the same thing as becoming suicidal: people in captivity live constantly with the fantasy of suicide, and occasional suicide attempts are not inconsistent with a general determination to survive … The wish for suicide in these extreme circumstances [is] a sign of resistance and pride. The stance of suicide is active: it preserves an inner sense of control … The captive asserts his defiance by his willingness to end his life."

Notes to Chapter 4. Escape and Rescue Operations

33. Philip Hallie, *The Paradox of Cruelty* (Weslayan University Press, 1969), 159.

34. I was subjected to sixty-six electroshock treatments. Larkin was not including the first sixteen treatments from the summer of 1965.

35. The book had been published in 1963 but was not as widely known as the movie.

36. David Rosenhan, "On Being Sane in Insane Places," *Science*, 179 (1973): 250–8. Rosenhan's article is available as a .pdf file in many

different locations on the internet, for example, http://psychrights.org /articles/rosenham.htm (accessed September 14, 2014).

37. Private email, November 9, 2012.

38. Serentil is a phenothiazine with side effects similar to Thorazine, http://www.drugs.com/pro/serentil.html (accessed September 6, 2014). Vivactil, http://tinyurl.com/njs54hq (accessed September 6, 2014) is a tricyclic antidepressant.

Notes to Chapter 5. *The Catching Up Years*

39. Irwin Levine and Toni Wine, "They say some people get married in the park on Sunday afternoon," from the song "What are you doing Sunday?" Sung by Tony Orlando and Dawn, released on the album *Candida,* 1970, http://www.youtube.com/watch?v=FXLQzYH_Owk (accessed September 20, 2014).

40. Daniel S. Schechter et al., "Is Maternal PTSD Associated with Greater Exposure of Very Young Children to Violent Media?" *Journal of Traumatic Stress* 22, 6 (2009): 658-662, http://tinyurl.com/n6phqxp (accessed September 6, 2014).

Notes to Chapter 6. *Falling Apart ...*

41. Long term use of Thorazine causes elevated levels of cholesystokinin, a factor stimulating the formation of gallstones.

42. Sang-Woo Woo and Sang-Hwan Do, "Tongue Laceration during Electroconvulsive Therapy," *Korean Journal of Anesthesiology,* Jan. 2012; 62 (1): 101–102, http://www.ncbi.nlm.nih.gov/pmc/articles/PMC3272 521/ (accessed September 6, 2014).

43. Steven Taylor, *Clinician's Guide to PTSD: A Cognitive-Behavioral Approach* (Guilford Press, 2009), 16, notes that one of the hallmarks of PTSD is exaggerated startled response.

44. The gynecologist assured me that my emotional reactions to the surgery and the accompanying PTSD symptoms could not be attributed to menopause, since the hysterectomy was only a partial one, leaving the ovaries and ovulation unaffected.

45. Since it was first included as an official diagnostic category in 1980, the definition of PTSD has broadened, and the condition is now seen as much more common than originally thought, occurring more than twice as often in women than in men. Matthew J. Friedman, MD, PhD, "PTSD History and Overview," US Department of Veterans Affairs,

http://www.ptsd .va.gov/professional/PTSD-overview/ptsd-overview.asp (accessed September 6, 2014).

46. Concluding his interpretation of the tests administered on June 10, 1965, the psychologist wrote, "The question of whether beneath this there exists a borderline schizophrenic illness is one that I am afraid I cannot answer with even reasonable certainty. I cannot be certain because the data are certainly not sufficiently extreme. I do think that it is likely that a borderline schizophrenic illness is at the root of this problem and I think this is particularly true since such an illness tends to show itself with severe depressive symptoms in teen age youngsters, and these certainly are present."

47. *Diagnostic and Statistical Manual of Mental Disorders, Fifth Edition: DSM-5,* 286-289.

48. Corrie ten Boom, *The Hiding Place* (Chosen Books, 1971).

Notes to Chapter 7. ... and Being Put Back Together

49. The Catholic Mass, Preparation for Communion. Based on Matthew 8:8: "And the centurion making answer, said: Lord, I am not worthy that thou shouldst enter under my roof: but only say the word, and my servant shall be healed."

50. Alla Renee Bozarth, *Life is Goodbye Life is Hello: Grieving Well through All Kinds of Loss* (Hazelden, 1994); first published in 1982.

51. Ronnie Janoff-Bulman, *Shattered Assumptions: Towards a New Psychology of Trauma* (The Free Press, 1992).

52. Thomas Keating, one of the chief writers on centering prayer, provides a good description of the practice in his book *Open Mind, Open Heart* (Continuum, 2006), first published in 1986. See also the website http://www.contemplativeoutreach.org/fr-thomas-keating (accessed September 6, 2014).

53. René Girard, *The Scapegoat,* translated by Yvonne Freccero (Johns Hopkins University Press, 1986), originally published as *Le bouc émissaire* (Paris: B. Grasset, 1982).

54. René Girard, *Job, the Victim of His People* (Stanford University Press, 1987), originally published as *La Route antique des hommes pervers* (Paris: B. Grasset, 1985), 35, notes, "The victim must participate if there is to be perfect unanimity. His voice must be joined to the unanimous voice of condemnation."

55. Colloquium on Violence and Religion (COV&R), http://www.uibk .ac.at/theol/cover/ (accessed September 6, 2014).

Notes to Chapter 8. Restorative Justice or Stalemate?

56. Howard Zehr, "Restoring Justice," *The Other Side* (Sept.-Dec, 1997).

57. Irving Goffman, *Stigma: Notes on the Management of Spoiled Identity* (Simon & Schuster, Inc., 1963).

Notes to Chapter 9. Two Adjustments and a Diagnosis

58. Goffmann, 14.

59. Paul Smith, "A Doubly Divisible Nearly Kirkman System," *Discrete Mathematics* 18 (1977): 93-96 writes that Laura's duplicate bridge schedule, published in 1961, was "the only example previously known of such a design with k>2." Laura's formula appears in G. W. Beynon, *Bridge Director's Manual* for Duplicate Games (G. Coffin, 1961), 149. *The ACBL Handbook of Rules and Regulations*, http://web2.acbl.org /handbook/handbook/chapter4.htm (accessed September 6, 2014), defines a movement as "the method of progression during the game, indicating the seat to be occupied and the boards to be played by each player at each round." These movements require complicated algorithms since every pair of players must play the same hands during the course of the competition.

60. Miroslav Volf, *The End of Memory: Remembering Rightly in a Violent World* (Eerdmans, 2006), 29; 34-35. Volf seeks to meet the challenges posed in remember wrongdoing: "It is essential to explore ways of redeeming memories of wrongs suffered. What does it take to remember for good, to remember in salutary rather than destructive ways? How can we help memory become a bridge between adversaries instead of a deep and dark ravine that separates them? How can former enemies remember together so as to reconcile, and how can they reconcile so as to remember together? These questions, I believe, pose the most important challenges to remembering in our conflict-ridden world."

Notes to Chapter 10. Triggers and Cancer Treatment

61. National Institute of Mental Health, "What is Post-traumatic Stress Disorder (PTSD)?" http://goo.gl/xgOkMg (accessed September 6, 2014).

62. Annmarie Huppert, Seattle PTSD Examiner, "PTSD Symptoms: The aftereffect of triggers," http://www.examiner.com/article/ptsd-symptoms-the-aftereffect-of-triggers (accessed September 6, 2014), lists examples of secondary wounding: "Disbelief – doubting or distrusting; Denial – refusing to believe; Discounting – dismissing or minimizing through comparisons or out-right statements; Blaming the survivor – on some level, suspecting the survivor deserved it; Stigmatization – judging the survivor negatively for normal reactions to the trauma or long-term symptoms; Denial of assistance – withholding necessary, expected services based on a personal or procedural judgment of the survivor's need or lack of entitlement."

63. *Diagnostic and Statistical Manual of Mental Disorders, Fifth Edition: DSM-5*, 271.

64. R-EPOCH involves the use of Rituximab, Etoposide, Prednisone, Oncovin, Cyclophosphamide, and Hydroxydaunorubicin, http://tinyurl .com/q8w9ywe (accessed September 6, 2014). Generally, patients receiving R-EPOCH chemotherapy undergo six to eight inpatient stays of five days each.

65. Stem cell transplants were not offered in Austin until February 2014.

66. Several of the drugs used either as chemotherapy infusions or as premedications to prevent anaphylaxis can cause hallucinations or other symptoms of psychosis. For example, Thankamma V. Ajithkumar et al., "Ifosfamide Encephalopathy," *Clinical Oncology* 19, 2 (2007): 108-114, http://goo.gl/4Fyg8L (accessed September 14, 2014), note that approximately 50% of patients receiving ifosfamide, one of the drugs used in the mobilization chemotherapy phase of stem cell transplants, develop varying degrees of encephalopathy ranging from fatigue and difficulty concentrating to hallucinations, psychotic delirium or worse.

67. Since a PET scan showed lymphoma responding well to chemotherapy, I was able to have an *autologous* stem cell transplant, one in which the patient is his own source of the stem cells. An *allogeneic* transplant uses donated cells from another person, requiring long-term pharmacological immunosuppression to counter the risk of rejection.

68. "Come back Silly Girl" was written by Barry Mann, and released as a single in 1960, sung by Steve Lawrence. In 1962, The Lettermen included the song on their album, *A Song for Young Love,* http://tinyurl.com/nbewmrp (accessed September 14, 2014) and it became a hit. My lyrics to the slightly altered tune were: "Come back stem cells, come back to me. / Find your place on the bone marrow tree, / o-o-o-o-o-o-o-o-o, come back to me. // Dig your roots down firm and deep /

Take a nap and get a little sleep / Sleepy little stem cells, whirled around in centrifuge / Dizzy, shocked and quite confused / Frozen into hibernation / Longing for your home! // Grow your patterns steadily / On that good old bone marrow tree / What will you grow up to be, / Little stem cells on the bone marrow tree? / White cells, red cells, platelets, and more / Macrophages, basophils, eosiniphils, / And lots and lots of Neutrophils, / And all of these cells all cancer free / From that grand old bone marrow tree. // Come back stem cells, Come back to me. / Find your place in the bone marrow tree. / I am waiting patiently. / Come back. / Come back. / Come soon!" I suggested to the nurses that they sing it in close harmony and use it for a charity benefit to request donations for the stem cell unit.

69. During the early recovery period, stem cell transplant recipients must go to the emergency room if their temperature reaches 100.4° F.

Notes to Chapter 11. New Beginnings

70. Joseph Dan, *Jewish Mysticism and Jewish Ethics* (University of Washington Press, 1986), paraphrased in Gail A. Hornstein, *To Redeem One Person Is to Redeem the World: The Life of Frieda Fromm Reichmann* (The Free Press, 2000), xvi.

71. Don Weitz, "Electroshocking Elderly People: Another Psychiatric Abuse," *Changes: An International Journal of Psychology and Psychotherapy* 15, 2 (1997), http://www.ect.org/resources/elderly.html (accessed September 6, 2014).

72. 2 Timothy 4:16-17: "At my first defense no one stood by me, but all were against me. May it not be held against them. But the Lord stood by me and gave me strength... And I was rescued from the lion's mouth." Cf. Psalm 22:21: "Save me from the lion's mouth."